Landed
King Haakon Bay
May 10, 1916

SOUTH GEORGIA I.

W9-CDD-620

SOUTH
SANDWICH
ISLANDS

ATLANTIC OCEAN

SEA

LOOSE PACK ICE

SOUTH POLE

WEDDELL SEA

Christmas Day, 1914

SOLID PACK ICE

ANTARCTIC CIRCLE

Cleared the Pack
Jan. 9, 1915

ENDURANCE Beset
Jan. 18

Caird Coast

QUEEN MAUD LAND

Sea Watches Canceled Feb. 24

SHACKLETON'S
VALIANT
VOYAGE

Sir Ernest Shackleton, 1915.

SHACKLETON'S VALIANT VOYAGE

by ALFRED LANSING

Illustrated with photographs

McGraw-Hill Book Company
New York   Toronto   London

CONTENTS

PREFACE

The story of Shackleton's voyage is one of almost incredible courage, hardship and fortitude. Since the appearance of the original *Endurance*, many requests for a shortened version have come from people working with teenagers and from young people themselves who have special enthusiasm for heroic adventure—the more inspiring in the case of Shackleton because the story is true. This book is the result.

Essentially, this book differs from the longer version only insofar as the lengthy historical background material has been omitted.

Every effort has been made to portray the events exactly as they occurred, and to record as accurately as possible the reactions of the men who lived them.

For this purpose, a wealth of material was generously made available to me, most notably the painstakingly detailed diaries of virtually every expedition member who kept one. In all cases, the exact language, punctuation and spelling have been preserved just as they were originally written.

I should like to take this opportunity again to pay my thanks to all the people who helped make this book possible, most especially the living survivors of the expedition, without whose interest, patience and cooperation there would be no book. I am very grateful.

Members of the Imperial Trans-Antarctic Expedition

Sir Ernest Shackleton   leader
Frank Wild   second-in-command
Frank Worsley   captain
Lionel Greenstreet   first officer
Hubert T. Hudson   navigator
Thomas Crean   second officer
Alfred Cheetham   third officer
Louis Rickenson   first engineer
A. J. Kerr   second engineer
Dr. Alexander H. Macklin   surgeon
Dr. James A. McIlroy   surgeon
James M. Wordie   geologist
Leonard D. A. Hussey   meteorologist
Reginald W. James   physicist
Robert S. Clark   biologist
James Francis Hurley   official photographer
George E. Marston   official artist
Thomas H. Orde-Lees   motor expert (later storekeeper)
Harry McNeish   carpenter
Charles J. Green   cook
Walter How   able seaman
William Bakewell   able seaman
Timothy McCarthy   able seaman
Thomas McLeod   able seaman
John Vincent   able seaman
Ernest Holness   fireman
William Stevenson   fireman
Perce Blackboro   stowaway (later steward)

1

Abandon Ship

THE ORDER to abandon ship was given at 5 P.M. For most of the men, however, no order was needed because by then everybody knew that the ship was done and that it was time to give up trying to save her. There was no show of fear or even apprehension. They had fought unceasingly for three days and they had lost. They accepted their defeat almost apathetically. They were simply too tired to care.

Frank Wild, the second-in-command, made his way forward along the buckling deck to the crew's quarters. There, two seamen, Walter How and William Bakewell, were lying in the lower bunks. Both were very nearly exhausted from almost three days at the pumps; yet they were unable to sleep because of the sounds the ship was making.

She was being crushed. Not all at once, but slowly, a little at a time. The pressure of ten million tons of ice was driving in against her sides. And dying as she was, she cried in agony. Her frames and planking, her immense timbers, many of them almost a foot thick, screamed as the killing pressure mounted. And when her timbers could no longer stand the strain, they broke with a report like artillery fire.

9

Most of the forecastle beams had already gone earlier in the day, and the deck was heaved upward and working slowly up and down as the pressure came and went.

Wild put his head inside the crew's quarters. He spoke quietly. "She's going, boys. I think it's time to get off." Seamen How and Bakewell rose from their bunks, picked up two pillowcases in which they had stowed some personal gear, and followed Wild back up on deck.

Wild next went down into the ship's tiny engine room. Kerr, the second engineer, was standing at the foot of the ladder, waiting. With him was Rickenson, the chief engineer. They had been below for almost seventy-two hours maintaining steam in the boilers to operate the engine-room pumps. During that time, though they couldn't actually see the ice in motion, they were altogether aware of what it was doing to the ship. Periodically her sides—though they were 2 feet thick in most places—bowed inward 6 inches under the pressure. Simultaneously, the steel floor plates jammed together, screeching where their edges met, then buckling up and suddenly overriding one another with a sharp metallic report.

Wild did not pause long. "Let down your fires," he said. "She's going." Kerr looked relieved.

Wild turned aft to the propeller shaftway. There McNeish, the old ship's carpenter, and McLeod, a seaman, were busy with torn pieces of blankets, calking a hastily built bulkhead thrown up in an attempt to stem the flow of water coming into the ship where the rudder and the sternpost had been torn out by the ice. But the water now was almost up to the floor plates, and it was gaining faster than the dam could hold it back and faster than the pumps could carry it away. Whenever the pressure ceased for a moment, there was the sound of the water running forward and filling up the hold.

Wild signaled to the two men to give up. Then he climbed the ladder to the main deck.

Clark, Hussey, James, and Wordie had been at the pumps but they had quit on their own, realizing the futility of what they were doing. Now they sat on cases of stores or on the deck itself, and leaned against the bulwarks. Their faces showed the unspeakable toil of the past three days at the pumps.

Farther forward, the dog-team drivers had attached a large piece of canvas to the port rail and made it into a sort of chute down to the ice alongside the ship. They took the forty-nine huskies from their kennels and slid each one down to other men waiting below. Ordinarily, any activity of this sort would have driven the dogs mad with excitement, but somehow they seemed to sense that something very extraordinary was going on. Not one fight broke out among them, and not a single dog attempted to break away.

It was, perhaps, the attitude of the men. They worked with a deliberate urgency, hardly speaking to one another. There was no display of alarm, however. In fact, apart from the movement of the ice and the sounds from the ship, the scene was one of relative calm. The temperature was 8½ degrees below zero, and a light southerly wind was blowing. Overhead, the twilight sky was clear.

But somewhere, far away to the south, a gale was blowing toward them. Though it probably wouldn't reach their position for at least two days, its approach was indicated by the movement of the ice, which stretched as far as the eye could see, and for hundreds of miles beyond that. So immense was the pack, and so tight, that though the gale had not yet reached them, the distant pressure of its winds was already crushing the floes together.

The whole surface of the ice was a chaos of movement. It looked like an enormous jigsaw puzzle composed of an uncountable number of ice floes—floating pieces of pack ice—some as small as a kitchen table and others a mile or more in diameter. These pieces, stretching away to in finity, were being shoved and crunched together by some invisible but irresistible force. The impression of the titanic power of the pack was heightened by the unhurried deliberateness of its motion. Wherever two thick floes came together, their edges butted and ground against one another for a time. Then, when neither of them showed signs of yielding, they rose, slowly and often quiveringly, driven by the implacable power behind them. Sometimes they would stop abruptly as the unseen force affecting the ice appeared mysteriously to lose interest. More frequently, though, the two floes—often 10 feet thick or more—would continue to rise, tenting up, until one or both of them broke and toppled over, creating a pressure ridge.

There were the sounds of the ice pack in movement—the basic noises, the grunting and whining of the floes, along with an occasional thud as a heavy block collapsed.

But in addition, the pack under compression seemed to have an almost limitless repertoire of other sounds, many of which seemed strangely unrelated to the noise of ice undergoing pressure. Sometimes there was a sound like a gigantic train with squeaky axles being shunted roughly about with a great deal of bumping and clattering. At the same time a huge ship's whistle blew, mingling with the crowing of roosters, the roar of a distant surf, the soft throb of an engine far away, and the moaning cries of an old woman. In the rare periods of calm, when the movement of the pack subsided for a moment, the muffled rolling of drums drifted across the air.

In this universe of ice, nowhere was the movement greater or the pressure more intense than in the floes that were attacking the ship. Nor could her position have been worse. One floe was jammed solidly against her starboard bow, and another held her on the same side aft. A third floe drove squarely in on her port beam opposite. Thus the ice was working to break her in half, directly amidships. On several occasions she bowed to starboard along her entire length.

Forward, where the worst of the onslaught was concentrated, the ice was inundating her. It piled higher and higher against her bows as she repelled each new wave, until gradually it mounted to her bulwarks, then crashed across the deck, overwhelming her with a crushing load that pushed her head down even deeper. Thus held, she was even more at the mercy of the floes driving against her flanks.

The ship reacted to each fresh wave of pressure in a

13

different way. Sometimes she simply quivered briefly as a human being might wince if seized by a single, stabbing pain. Other times she retched in a series of convulsive jerks accompanied by anguished outcries. On these occasions her three masts whipped violently back and forth as the rigging tightened like harpstrings. But most agonizing for the men were the times when she seemed a huge creature suffocating and gasping for breath, her sides heaving against the strangling pressure.

More than any other single impression in those final hours, all the men were struck, almost to the point of horror, by the way the ship behaved like a giant beast in its death agonies.

By 7 P.M., all essential gear had been transferred to the ice, and a camp of sorts had been established on a solid floe a short distance to starboard. The three lifeboats—one whaleboat and two square-sterned cutters—had been lowered the night before. As they went over the side onto the ice, most of the men felt immense relief at being away from the doomed ship, and few if any of them would have returned to her voluntarily.

However, a few unfortunate souls were ordered back to retrieve various items. One was Alexander Macklin, a stocky young physician, who also happened to be the driver of a dog team. He had just tethered his dogs at the camp when he was told to go with Wild to get some lumber out of the ship's forehold.

The two men started out and had just reached the ship when a great shout went up from the campsite. The floe

14

on which the tents were pitched was itself breaking up. Wild and Macklin rushed back. The teams were harnessed and the tents, stores, sledges, and all the gear were hurriedly moved to another floe a hundred yards farther from the ship.

By the time the transfer was completed, the ship seemed on the point of going under, so the two men hurried to get aboard. They picked their way among the blocks of ice littering the forecastle, then lifted a hatch leading down into the forepeak. The ladder had been wrenched from its supports and had fallen to one side. To get down, they had to lower themselves hand over hand into the darkness.

The noise inside was indescribable. The half-empty compartment, like a giant sounding box, amplified every snapping bolt and splintering timber. From where they stood, the sides of the ship were only a few feet away, and they could hear the ice outside battering to break through.

They waited for a moment until their eyes grew accustomed to the gloom, and what they saw then was terrifying. The uprights were caving in and the cross members overhead were on the verge of going. It looked as if some giant vise were being applied to the ship and slowly tightened until she could no longer hold out against its pressure.

The lumber they were after was stored in the black-dark recesses of the side pockets in the very bow of the ship. To reach it, they had to crawl through a thwartships bulkhead, and they could see that the bulkhead itself bulged outward as if it might burst at any moment, causing the whole forecastle to collapse around them.

Macklin hesitated for just a moment, and Wild, sensing the other's fear, shouted to him above the noise of the ship to stay where he was. Then Wild plunged through the opening and a few minutes later began passing boards out to Macklin.

The two men worked with feverish speed, but even so the job seemed interminable. Macklin was sure they would never get the last board out in time. But finally Wild's head reappeared through the opening. They hoisted the lumber up on deck, climbed out, and stood for a long moment without speaking, savoring the exquisite feeling of safety. Later, to the privacy of his diary, Macklin confided: "I do not think I have ever had such a horrible sickening sensation of fear as I had whilst in the hold of that breaking ship."

Within an hour after the last man was off, the ice pierced her sides. Sharp spears drove through first, opening wounds that let in whole blocks and chunks of floes. Everything from midships forward was now submerged. The entire starboard side of the deckhouse had been crushed by the ice with such force that some empty gasoline cans stacked on deck had been shoved through the deckhouse wall and halfway across to the other side, carrying before them a large framed picture that had hung on the wall. Somehow, the glass on its front had not broken.

Later, after things had settled down at the camp, a few

men returned to look at the derelict that had been their ship. But not many. Most of them huddled in their tents, cold through and tired, for the time being indifferent to their fate.

The general feeling of relief at being off the ship was not shared by one man—at least not in the larger sense. He was a thickset individual with a wide face and a broad nose, and he spoke with a trace of an Irish brogue. During the hours it took to abandon the ship, he had remained more or less apart as the equipment, dogs, and men were gotten off.

His name was Sir Ernest Shackleton, and the twenty-seven men he had watched so ingloriously leaving their stricken ship were the members of his Imperial Trans-Antarctic Expedition.

The date was October 27, 1915. The name of the ship was *Endurance*. The position was 69°5′ South, 51°30′ West—deep in the icy wasteland of the Antarctic's treacherous Weddell Sea, just about midway between the South Pole and the nearest known outpost of humanity, some 1,200 miles away.

Few men have borne the responsibility Shackleton did at that moment. Though he certainly was aware that their situation was desperate, he could not possibly have conceived then the physical and emotional demands that ultimately would be placed upon them, the rigors they would have to endure, the sufferings to which they would be subjected.

They were for all practical purposes alone in Antarctica. It had been very nearly a year since they had last

17

been in contact with civilization. Nobody in the outside world knew they were in trouble, much less where they were. They had no radio transmitter with which to notify any would-be rescuers, and it is safe to say that no rescuers could have reached them even if the castaways had been able to broadcast an SOS. It was 1915, and there were no helicopters, no Weasels, no Sno-Cats, no suitable planes.

And of course the *Endurance* was finished. This magnificent piece of shipbuilding, 144 feet long, launched only three years before as a glistening auxiliary-powered barkentine and considered very probably the strongest wooden ship ever built anywhere . . . was done. For nine months, ever since the previous January when she was trapped in the ice, she had staunchly held out against the pressure of the pack. Yet in the end the ice had won. Even though her sides were more than two feet thick in most places and reinforced with double the number of frames in a conventional ship, it was not enough—not against the fantastic pressures of the Weddell Sea pack ice.

And so she was done, leaving her twenty-eight men in a situation that was starkly terrifying in its simplicity: If they were to get out—they had to get themselves out.

The Palmer Peninsula, the nearest known land, they estimated to be 182 miles WSW of them (though actually it was closer to 210 miles). But the Palmer Peninsula was inhabited by neither human beings nor animals, and offered them nothing in the way of relief or rescue.

The nearest known place where they might at least find food and shelter was tiny Paulet Island, less than a mile and a half in diameter, which lay 346 miles northwest across the heaving pack ice. There, in 1903, twelve years before, the crew of a Swedish ship had spent the winter after their vessel, the *Antarctic,* had been crushed by the Weddell Sea ice. The ship which finally rescued that party deposited its stock of stores on Paulet Island for the use of any later castaways. Ironically, it was Shackleton himself who had been commissioned at the time to purchase those stores—and now, a dozen years later, it was he who needed them.

2

Challenge

SHACKLETON'S ORDER to abandon ship, while it signaled the beginning of the greatest of all Antarctic adventures, also sealed the fate of one of the most ambitious of all Antarctic expeditions. The goal of the Imperial Trans-Antarctic Expedition, as its name implies, was to cross the Antarctic continent overland from west to east.

Evidence of the scope of such an undertaking is the fact that after Shackleton's failure, the crossing of the continent remained untried for fully forty-three years—until 1957–1958. Then, as an independent enterprise conducted during the International Geophysical Year, Dr. Vivian E. Fuchs led the Commonwealth Trans-Antarctic Expedition on the trek. And even Fuchs, though his party was equipped with heated, tracked vehicles and powerful radios, and guided by reconnaissance planes and dog teams, was strongly urged to give up. It was only after a tortuous journey lasting nearly four months that Fuchs did in fact achieve what Shackleton set out to do in 1915.

This was Shackleton's third expedition to the Antarctic. He had gone first in 1901 as a member of the National Antarctic Expedition led by Robert F. Scott.

Then in 1907, Shackleton led the first expedition actually to declare the Pole as its goal. With three companions, Shackleton struggled to within 97 miles of their destination and then had to turn back because of a shortage of food. The return journey was a desperate race with death. But the party finally made it, and Shackleton returned to England a hero of the Empire. He wrote a book, and he went on a worldwide lecture tour. But even before it was over, his thoughts had returned to the Antarctic.

And so the plan was born. It was Shackleton's idea to take a ship into the Weddell Sea and land a sledging party of six men and seventy dogs near Vahsel Bay, approximately 78° South, 36° West. At more or less the same time, a second ship would put into McMurdo Sound in the Ross Sea, almost directly across the continent from the Weddell Sea base. The Ross Sea party was to set down a series of food caches from their base almost to the Pole. While this was being done, the Weddell Sea group would be sledging toward the Pole, living on their own rations. From the Pole they would proceed to the vicinity of the mighty Beardmore Glacier, where they would replenish their supplies at the southernmost depot laid down by the Ross Sea party. Other caches of rations along the route would keep them supplied until they arrived at the McMurdo Sound base.

Such was the plan on paper, and it was typical of Shackleton—purposeful, bold, and neat. He had not the slightest doubt that the expedition would achieve its goal.

The whole undertaking was criticized in some circles

21

as being too "audacious." And perhaps it was. But if it hadn't been audacious, it wouldn't have been to Shackleton's liking. He was, above all, an explorer in the classic mold—utterly self-reliant, romantic, and just a little swashbuckling.

He was now forty years old, of medium height and thick of neck, with broad, heavy shoulders a trifle stooped, and dark brown hair parted in the center. He had a wide, sensuous but expressive mouth that could curl into a laugh or tighten into a thin fixed line with equal facility. His jaw was like iron. His gray-blue eyes, like his mouth, could come alight with fun or darken into a steely and frightening gaze. His face was handsome, though it often wore a brooding expression—as if his thoughts were somewhere else—which gave him at times a kind of darkling look. He had small hands, but his grip was strong and confident. He spoke softly and somewhat slowly in an indefinite baritone, with just the recollection of a brogue from his County Kildare birth.

Whatever his mood—whether it was gay and breezy, or dark with rage—he had one pervading characteristic: he was purposeful.

Temperamentally, Shackleton almost needed the Antarctic—something so enormous, so demanding, that it provided a touchstone for his monstrous ego and implacable drive. In ordinary situations, Shackleton's tremendous capacity for boldness and daring found almost nothing worthy of its pulling power; he was a Percheron draft horse harnessed to a child's wagon cart. But in the

Antarctic—here was a burden which challenged every atom of his strength.

Thus, while Shackleton was undeniably out of place, even inept, in a great many everyday situations, he had a talent—a genius, even—that he shared with only a handful of men throughout history—genuine leadership. He was, as one of his men put it, "the greatest leader that ever came on God's earth, bar none." For all his blind spots and inadequacies, Shackleton merited this tribute:

> "For scientific leadership give me Scott; for swift and efficient travel, Amundsen; but when you are in a hopeless situation, when there seems no way out, get down on your knees and pray for Shackleton."

This, then, was the man who developed the idea of crossing the Antarctic continent—on foot.

Shackleton set out on his ambitious trans-Antarctic undertaking with a crew list containing twenty-seven names, including his own. But actually the party was made up of twenty-eight men, for there had been an uninvited guest. He was a stocky eighteen-year-old Welshman named Perce Blackboro. He had stowed away at Buenos Aires, where the *Endurance* stopped briefly before sailing to the desolate island of South Georgia, their last port of call before leaving for Antarctica. By the time he was discovered, the ship was too far from land to put him ashore again, and so he was signed on as a regular member of the expedition.

The men themselves were divided roughly into three

groups: the officers and seamen who would man the ship; the team of scientists who were to study the weather conditions, geology, and marine life in the areas visited; and finally the members of the actual trans-continental party.

However, not one of these three tasks was ever to be performed. The *Endurance* was caught in the ice and never approached closer than 60 miles to the shore of Antarctica. And on October 27, 1915, when the ice had finally wrecked the ship beyond hope of salvation, the seamen were left with no vessel to sail; the scientists had almost no means for making any of their studies; and all thought of crossing the continent had to be abandoned, along with the *Endurance*.

In fact, the only task that remained was to survive and somehow reach civilization once more.

3

The March Begins

MAY THE LORD HELP YOU to do your duty & guide you through all the dangers by land and sea.

"May you see the Works of the Lord & all His Wonders in the deep."

These words were written on the flyleaf of a Bible given to the expedition by Queen Mother Alexandra of England. Shackleton carried the Bible in his hand as he left the *Endurance* and walked slowly across the ice toward the campsite.

The others hardly noticed his arrival. They were busy crawling in and out of the tents, trying, numbly, to create some degree of comfort with what energy remained in them. Some arranged pieces of lumber to keep themselves off the snow-covered ice. Others spread pieces of canvas as ground covers. But there was not enough flooring for everybody and several men had to lie directly on the bare snow. It made little difference. Sleep was all that mattered. And they slept—most of them embracing their nearest tentmates to keep from freezing.

When morning came, the men turned out stiff and

cold from sleeping on the ice. After a time they turned to the job of sorting out equipment and stowing it securely on the sledges. It was a quiet time; everyone understood his job and went about it without having to be told.

The plan, as they all knew, was to march toward Paulet Island, 346 miles to the northwest, where the stores left in 1903 should still be. The distance was farther than from New York City to Pittsburgh, Pennsylvania, and they would be dragging two of their three boats with them, since it was assumed that they would eventually run into open water.

Old Harry McNeish, the carpenter, and Thomas McLeod, a seaman, began mounting the whaler and one of the two cutters onto sledges. The boats with their sledges would weigh more than a ton apiece, and everybody was thoroughly aware just how difficult it was going to be dragging them over the chaotic surface of the ice, with its pressure ridges occasionally twenty feet high.

Nevertheless, there was a remarkable absence of discouragement. Their attitude was a combination of dazed fatigue and relief. Nobody paused to reflect on the terrible consequences of losing their ship. Nor were they upset by the fact that they were now camped on a piece of ice perhaps 6 feet thick. It was a haven compared with the nightmare of labor and uncertainty of the last few days on the *Endurance*. Just then it was quite enough to be alive—and they were merely doing what they had to do to stay that way.

There was even a trace of mild exhilaration in their

attitude. Now, at least, they had a clear-cut task ahead of them. The nine months of indecision, of speculation about what might happen, of aimless drifting with the pack were over. Now they simply had to get themselves out, however appallingly difficult that might be.

The work of packing the sledges continued the next day, and early in the afternoon Shackleton called all hands together into the center of the circle of tents. His face was grave. He explained it was imperative that all weight be reduced to the barest minimum. Each man, he said, would be allowed the clothes on his back, plus two pairs of mittens, six pairs of socks, two pairs of boots, a sleeping bag, a pound of tobacco—and two pounds of personal gear. Speaking with the utmost conviction, Shackleton pointed out that no article was of any value when weighed against their ultimate survival, and he exhorted them to be ruthless in ridding themselves of every unnecessary ounce, regardless of its value.

After he had spoken, he reached under his parka and took out a gold cigarette case and several gold sovereigns and threw them into the snow at his feet.

Then he opened the Bible Queen Alexandra had given them and ripped out the flyleaf and the page containing the Twenty-third Psalm. He also tore out the page from the Book of Job with this verse on it:

"Out of whose womb came the ice?
  And the hoary frost of Heaven, who hath gendered it?
  The waters are hid as with a stone.
  And the face of the deep is frozen."

Then he laid the Bible in the snow and walked away.

It was a dramatic gesture, but that was the way Shackleton wanted it. From studying the outcome of past expeditions, he believed that those that burdened themselves with equipment to meet every contingency had fared much worse than those that had sacrificed total preparedness for speed.

As the afternoon wore on, the number of nonessentials dumped in the snow grew steadily. It was an "extraordinary collection of stuff," Reginald James noted in his diary. Chronometers, axes, an ophthalmoscope, saws, telescopes, socks, lenses, jerseys, chisels, books, stationery —and a large number of pictures and personal keepsakes. For some men, the two-pound limit on personal gear was relaxed for special reasons. The expedition's two surgeons, of course, were permitted a small amount of medical supplies and instruments. The men with diaries were allowed to keep them. And Hussey, the meteorologist, actually was ordered to take his zither banjo along, even though it weighed 12 pounds. It was lashed in its case under the bow sheets of the whaler to keep it out of the weather.

The journey would begin the next day. On the eve of setting out, Shackleton wrote: "I pray God I can manage to get the whole party safe to civilization."

October 30 was gray and overcast with a bit of occasional wet snow. The temperature was an uncomfortably warm 15 degrees, which made the surface of the ice soft —far from ideal for sledging.

They spent the morning readying the last bit of stores.

About eleven-thirty, Shackleton, with Wild, went out to prospect for a route. Before he left, Shackleton ordered the three youngest puppies killed, along with Sirius, an older puppy from an earlier litter, whose only fault was that he had never been broken to harness. McNeish's tomcat, which had mistakenly been named Mrs. Chippy before his sex was determined, also was to be destroyed. There was only food for those who could pull their weight.

Tom Crean, a tough and practical individual who had been second officer aboard the *Endurance,* took the younger puppies and Mrs. Chippy some distance from camp and shot them without a qualm, but it was Macklin's duty to destroy Sirius, and he could hardly face the task. Reluctantly he got a 12-gauge shotgun from Wild's tent; then he led Sirius off toward a distant pressure ridge. When he found a suitable spot he stopped and stood over the little dog. Sirius was an eager, friendly puppy, and he kept jumping up, wagging his tail and trying to lick Macklin's hand. Macklin kept pushing him away until finally he got up nerve enough to put the shotgun to Sirius' neck. He pulled the trigger, but his hand was shaking so he had to reload and fire a second time to finish the puppy off.

The journey was begun about 2 P.M. Shackleton, Wordie, Hussey, and "Buddha" Hudson, the one-time navigator, went ahead with a sledge and an assortment of shovels and mountaineering pickaxes. They tried to guide the main party along a level route, but every few hundred yards it was necessary to cross a pressure ridge.

29

Then they set to work, chopping away at it until they had carved out a miniature mountain pass for the boats. On particularly high ridges, they had to build a ramp of ice and snow up one side and down the other.

The teams came next, pulling sledges loaded with up to 900 pounds apiece. The boats, drawn by fifteen men harnessed in traces under Worsley's command, were last. It was killing toil. Because of their weight, the boats sank into the soft surface of the snow. To move them, the men in the traces had to strain forward, at times leaning nearly parallel with the ground, and the whole operation was more like plowing than sledging. By 5 P.M., after three hours on the trail, they had progressed only one mile from the ship in a direct line.

Supper was at six o'clock, and the weary men immediately crawled into their sleeping bags. During the night it began to snow heavily, and by dawn there was a mushy 6-inch blanket. The temperature soared to 25 degrees, and as soon as they were on the trail they found it was torturously slow going.

About 4 P.M., having covered only a scant three-quarters of a mile, the party arrived at a thick, level floe. Since there wasn't another suitable camping place within sight, Shackleton decided they would stop for the night. Almost as fast as the tents were pitched, they were soaked inside. It was impossible to crawl into them without bringing in quantities of wet, clinging snow.

Macklin commented: "I cannot help feeling sorry for Worsley at the mouth of our tent, for he gets the wet brought in by everybody."

Worsley, however, was far from distressed. He wrote in his diary that same night: "The rapidity with which one can completely change one's ideas ... and accommodate ourselves to a state of barbarism is wonderful."

Shackleton was pleased by the general cheeriness of the men. "Many look on this as a spree," he recorded. "It is better so."

He also observed: "This floe really strong. Will sleep tonight."

The floe was indeed a giant, more than a half mile in diameter and made up of ice 10 feet thick, with 5 feet of snow on top of that. It was probably more than two years old, Worsley estimated.

Its sturdiness was very much on Shackleton's mind the following morning when he went out with Wild and Worsley to look for a route. They saw tumbled confusion to the west; "a sea of pressure," Shackleton declared, "impossible to advance." The boats and sledges would not last 10 miles over such a surface.

On the way back to camp, Shackleton came to a decision. When he arrived he called all hands together. He told the men that they had made less than a mile a day, and that the route ahead appeared to get progressively worse. Their advance, he said, hardly merited the effort it required. And since they were not likely to find a better place to camp, they would stay where they were until the drift of the ice should carry them closer to land.

There was a flicker of disappointment on several faces, but Shackleton allowed no time for regrets. He dispatched dog teams back to the original camp, a mile and three-quarters to the rear, to bring up all the food, clothing, and gear possible.

Wild, with six men, was sent back to the ship to salvage anything of value. They hacked a hole in the galley roof and recovered a few cases of stores.

For supper that night, Shackleton ordered Green, the cook, to put some lumps of blubber into the seal meat stew so that the party might get accustomed to eating it. Some of the men, when they saw the rubbery, cod-liver-oil-flavored chunks floating around in their stew-like ration of "hoosh," meticulously removed every trace. But the majority were so hungry they were delighted to gobble down every mouthful, blubber included.

4

Waiting

ALMOST SURPRISINGLY, they had been on the ice exactly one week. In seven short days they had gone from the well-ordered, even pleasant existence on board the *Endurance* to one of primitive discomfort, of unending wet and inescapable cold. A little more than a week before they had slept in their own warm bunks and eaten their meals in the cozy atmosphere around the mess table. Now they were crammed together in overcrowded tents, lying in reindeer or woolen sleeping bags on bare ice, or at best on odd pieces of hard lumber. At mealtimes, they sat in the snow, and each man ate out of an aluminum mug they called a pannican, into which everything was dumped at the same time. For utensils, each had a spoon, a knife —and his fingers.

They were castaways in one of the most savage regions of the world, drifting they knew not where, without a hope of rescue, subsisting only so long as Providence sent them food to eat.

And yet they had adjusted with surprisingly little trouble to their new life, and most of them were quite sincerely happy. The adaptability of the human creature is such that they actually had to remind themselves on occasion of their desperate circumstances. On November 4, Macklin wrote in his diary: "It has been a lovely day, and it is hard to think we are in a frightfully precarious situation."

It was an observation typical of the entire party. There was not a hero among them, at least not in the fictional sense. Still not a single diary reflected anything beyond the matter-of-fact routine of each day's business.

There was only one major change in their general outlook—their attitude toward food. Worsley had this to say: "It is scandalous—all we seem to live for and think of now is food. I have never in my life taken half such a keen interest in food as I do now—and we are all alike. ... We are ready to eat anything, especially cooked blubber which none of us would tackle before. Probably living totally in the open and having to rely on food instead of fire for body heat makes us think so much of food. . . ."

They were up at six the following morning, November 5, and nearly everyone returned to the ship. Several men attempted some personal salvage operations.

Lionel Greenstreet, who had been first officer on the *Endurance*, managed to get far enough into his cabin to secure a few books. How and Bakewell, whose quarters in the forecastle were hopelessly submerged, went treasure-hunting elsewhere. Carefully making their way along a passageway below, they passed the door of the compartment that Frank Hurley, the photographer, had used as a darkroom and rescued the cases containing Hurley's photographic negatives.

As a whole, the salvage party worked with abandon. The entire wheelhouse was removed as a unit and returned to camp to serve as a sort of portable storehouse. Lumber, spars, sails, and rigging followed.

But the amount of stores thus far salvaged from the ship was disappointingly small. Most of the provisions were below decks; to get at them would require tearing the deck away, and it was more than a foot thick in places and nearly 3 feet under water. But it was imperative that the stores be obtained, so the next day McNeish was put in charge, and after hours of work with ice chisels and various rigs of tackle the party wrenched and pried a hole through the deck.

Almost immediately, stores began to float up, beginning with a barrel of walnuts. Other supplies were grappled to the surface—a case of sugar, a boxful of baking soda. By the end of the day, nearly 3½ tons of flour, rice, sugar, barley, lentils, vegetables, and jam had been rescued and sledged back to camp.

Salvage work had to be suspended on the afternoon of November 6, when a southerly blizzard came up and drove the men into their tents. It was their first blizzard on the ice. The tents shook and rattled with the force of the gale, while the men huddled inside, cold and cramped. The only cheering thought was that the gale was driving them north—toward civilization, so infinitely far away.

Shackleton took the opportunity to evaluate their food situation. He reckoned their supplies would last three months at full rations. And since they were sure to get increasing numbers of seals and penguins, he decided it was safe to go on full rations for the next two months.

This would carry them into January, the midpoint of the Antarctic summer. By that time, Shackleton was sure, they would know what fate lay in store for them, and then the ultimate decision would have to be made while there was still time to act before the onslaught of winter.

The ice might continue to drift generally northwest, carrying them toward the Palmer Peninsula or the open sea. Or the pack might be arrested for some reason, and they would remain more or less in the same spot. Finally, the ice might veer northeast or even east, carrying them away from land.

Whatever happened, January would mark the point of no return. If the drift was toward land, they should have enough open water by then to launch the boats and make for the most promising spot. If the pack were to stop moving, then, rather than spend the winter camped on the ice, the party would make a dash for the nearest land. It would be a risky business, but better than wintering on the ice.

The third prospect was grim indeed. If the pack drifted northeast or east and if they were unable to launch the boats—they would have to spend the winter adrift on the floes, somehow attempting to survive the polar night with its paralyzing cold and violent storms. But nobody even cared to think much about such a possibility.

5

"She's Going . . ."

AS THE DAYS WORE ON, it was impossible to prevent a certain amount of complacency from arising as the men became increasingly accustomed to the well-established day-in, day-out routine of camp life. The line of pale-green tents seemed now almost as familiar as the ship had been.

Each day in camp began at 6:30 A.M., when the night watchman started the fire in the makeshift blubber stove Hurley had fashioned from an old oil drum. It sat in the center of the galley, which was itself little more than a makeshift windbreak, constructed of spars driven into the ice, over which pieces of sail had been stretched and lashed in place. A chronometer hung on one post and a mirror on another.

As soon as the stove was burning, the night watchman awakened Green to begin breakfast. By seven o'clock, the men had begun to emerge from their tents. Many carried frayed toothbrushes, and they brushed their teeth with snow.

After breakfast, the men went about their customary chores. Green spent the morning making "bannocks." These were lumps of fried flour, frequently mixed with dog pemmican (a concentrated meat-food) or lentils or anything that would give them some flavor. And there was always ice to be melted into water.

Old Chippy McNeish spent these days raising the sides of the whaler and one of the cutters to make them as seaworthy as possible. Hurley, too, was busy preparing for the boat journey. He was not only an excellent photographer but a skilled tinsmith as well, and he was now at work fashioning a primitive boat pump from a tubelike portion of the ship's compass binnacle.

The rest of the party spent their time hunting seals, and it was a bloody business. Ammunition for their three guns was limited, and as a result, the men killed the seals by hand whenever possible. This involved approaching the animal cautiously, then stunning it across the nose with a ski or a broken oar and cutting its jugular vein so that the animal bled to death.

In the beginning, a few of the men, particularly little Louis Rickenson, the chief engineer, were squeamish about this seemingly cold-blooded method of hunting. But not for long. The will to survive soon dispelled any hesitancy to obtain food by any means.

After lunch the men went to work strengthening sledge harnesses, repacking equipment, or helping with the boats. The dogs were fed at 5 P.M., and supper for the men was at five-thirty—most often seal hoosh, a bannock, and a mug of hot watered cocoa.

In the evenings, activities varied somewhat from tent to tent. There was the reading aloud in Worsley's tent. In No. 1, Shackleton's four-man tent, invariably there was a game of poker patience or bridge. The seamen and firemen in No. 4 tent also played cards or sat around "yarning." Whenever the subject of women was discussed, it was in a nostalgic sentimental way—of a longing to see a wife, a mother, or a sweetheart at home.

The official lights-out—a figure of speech since there was daylight now nearly sixteen hours a day—was at 8:30 P.M. A good many men turned in earlier, after removing their trousers and jerseys and possibly putting on a pair of dry socks. Nobody ever took off his underwear. Some men stayed up after the official curfew, though they had to talk in subdued voices. In the cold, crisp air, any noise carried an unusually long distance.

By 10 P.M. everything was quiet in the camp except for the lone night watchman, patrolling among the tents and keeping an eye on the galley chronometer which told him when his one-hour tour of duty was over.

During these three weeks since the *Endurance* had been abandoned, perhaps the most striking change in the party was their appearance. Some men had always worn beards, and they were now just a little shaggier than before. But faces that had previously been clean-shaven were now covered with a scrubby, half-inch growth of whiskers.

And everybody's face was growing progressively filthier from the blubber smoke. It infiltrated everywhere, clung tenaciously to whatever it touched, and responded poorly to snow and the small amount of soap that could be spared for washing.

There were two schools of thought on the matter of cleanliness. Though any over-all bathing was out of the

39

question, some men scrubbed their faces in snow whenever the weather permitted. Others purposely let the dirt accumulate on the theory that it would toughen their skin against frostbite.

Similarly, the camp was divided on the matter of eating into the savers and the nonsavers. Frank Worsley headed the nonsavers, who gobbled down anything they could get whenever they could get it. Orde-Lees, the storekeeper, who had an all-consuming fear of starving to death, was the leading advocate of the savers' school of thought. He rarely ate his entire ration at any meal. Instead, he stored a little piece of cheese or a bit of bannock somewhere in his clothing to be eaten later or saved for the leaner days he was sure would come. He could and did often produce from his pocket a lump of food that had been issued a week, two weeks, three weeks before.

Early on the morning of November 21, a salvage party went back to the ship. They noticed that the floes which had driven into her sides were moving slightly. They returned to camp and were unharnessing and feeding the dogs, when Shackleton came out to watch. He was standing close to Hurley's sledge. It was 4:50 P.M. Out of the corner of his eye he noticed the ship move. He turned quickly and saw her stack disappear behind a hummock.

"She's going, boys!" he shouted, and dashed up the lookout tower. A moment later all hands were out of the tents and scrambling to gain a vantage point. They watched in silence. Away across the pack, the stern of the *Endurance* rose 20 feet into the air and hung there for a moment with her motionless propeller and her smashed rudder held aloft. Then slowly, silently, she disappeared beneath the ice, leaving only a small gap of black, open water to mark where she had been. Within sixty seconds, even that was gone as the ice closed up again. It had all happened in ten minutes.

Shackleton that night noted simply in his diary that the *Endurance* was gone, and added: "I cannot write about it."

And so they were alone. Now, in every direction, there was nothing to be seen but the endless ice. Their position was 68°38½' South, 52°28' West—a place where no man had ever been before, nor could they conceive that any man would ever want to be again.

6

"Strike to Westward"

THE FINAL LOSS of the *Endurance* was a shock in that it severed what had seemed their last tie with civilization. It was a finality. The ship had been a symbol, a tangible, physical symbol that linked them with the outside world. She had brought them nearly halfway around the globe, or, as Worsley put it, ". . . carried us so far and so well and then put forth the bravest fight that ever a ship had fought before yielding to the remorseless pack." Now she was gone.

But the reaction was largely a sentimental one, as after the passing of an old friend who had been on the verge of death for a long time. They had been expecting her to go for weeks. When she had been abandoned twenty-five days before, it had seemed that she would sink at any moment. Indeed, it was remarkable that she had stayed on the surface so long. Her sinking was inevitable—and the inevitable had simply occurred.

Even in spite of the final loss of the *Endurance,* the men showed an astonishing optimism. The task of raising the whaler's sides was almost complete and everyone was impressed with the job McNeish had done. The shortage of tools and lack of materials seemed not to have handicapped him in the least. To calk the planks he had added, he had been forced to resort to cotton lamp wick and the oil colors from Marston's artist's box.

Now that the boats were ready, nothing remained except to name them, and Shackleton decided the honor should go to the expedition's principal backers. Accordingly, the whaler was christened the *James Caird;* the No. 1 cutter became the *Dudley Docker,* and the second cutter, the *Stancomb Wills.* George Marston, the artist, got busy with what remained of his paints and lettered the proper name on each boat.

Shackleton also adopted Worsley's suggestion that they call the floe on which they were established "Ocean Camp."

And so November was drawing to a close. They had been on the ice just a month. And for all the trials and discomforts, these weeks of primitive living had been peculiarly enriching. The men had been forced to develop a degree of self-reliance greater than they had ever imagined possible. After spending four hours sewing an elaborate patch on the seat of his only pair of trousers, Macklin wrote one day, "What an ingrate I have been for such jobs when done for me at home." Greenstreet felt much the same way after he had devoted several days to scraping and curing a piece of sealskin to resole his boots. He paused in the midst of his task to write in his diary: "One of the finest days we have ever had . . . a pleasure to be alive."

In some ways they had come to know themselves better. In this lonely world of ice and emptiness, they had achieved at least a limited kind of contentment. They had been tested and found not wanting.

The fact that the entire party had been kept occupied contributed much to their feeling of well-being. But toward the close of November, they simply began to run out of things to do. In effect, they had completed their part of the bargain. Now all that remained was for the ice to open.

But it didn't open. One day wore on into the next, and the pack remained substantially the same. Nor was their drift particularly satisfactory. During this period the winds had been southerly but never very strong, so the pack continued to move north at the same sluggish pace, about 2 miles a day.

Time, indeed, was beginning to weigh a little heavily. Each day blurred anonymously into the one before. Though they invariably tried to see the good side of things, they were unable to fight off a growing sense of disappointment. Macklin wrote on December 1: "We have done a degree [of latitude—60 miles] in less than a month. This is not as good as it might be, but we are gradually getting north, and so far everything is hopeful."

And on December 7, McNeish rationalized: "We have drifted back a bit, but I think it will be for our good as it will give the ice between us & the Land a chance to get out & us a chance in."

Since abandoning the *Endurance,* they had covered 80 miles in a straight line almost due north. But their drift had described a slight arc, which was now curving def-

44

initely to the east, away from land. Not enough to cause real worry, but enough to stir concern.

Shackleton had suffered a bad attack of sciatica which had kept him confined to his tent and more or less out of touch with things. But toward the middle of the month his condition improved and he became aware of the growing restiveness among the men. The situation was not improved on December 17. Just after they had drifted across the 67th parallel of latitude, the wind hauled around to the northeast. The next day's observation showed that they had been blown back across it.

An air of tension, of patience pushed too far, settled on the camp that night, and conversation was scant. Many of the men went to sleep right after supper.

Shackleton was concerned. Of all their enemies—the cold, the ice, the sea—he feared none more than demoralization. On December 19, he wrote in his diary: "Am thinking of starting off for the west."

The need for action was settled in his mind the next day, and he announced his plan that afternoon. He said that on the following morning, he would go with Wild, Hurley, and Crean's teams to survey the country to the west.

The reaction was immediate. Greenstreet wrote: "The Boss seems keen to try to strike to westward, as we don't make headway as we are. That will mean travelling light and taking only two boats at the most and leaving a lot of provisions behind. As far as I have seen the going will be awful, everything being in a state of softness far worse than when we left the ship, and in my opinion it would be a measure to be taken only as a last resort and I sincerely hope he will give up the idea directly. There have been great arguments about the matter in our tent. . . ."

Indeed there were. Worsley felt much the same way: "My idea is to stay here—unless the drift should become large to the East. . . . The advantages of waiting a little longer are that the drift will convey us part of our journey without any exertion on our part, that probably we should be able to keep 3 boats, and that in the meantime leads may open in the pack."

But a great many others defended Shackleton's decision warmly. As Macklin put it: ". . . personally I think that we ought to push west as hard as we can. We know that there is land 200 miles west, therefore the pack edge should be somewhere about 150–180 miles off in that direction. . . . At our present rate of drift it would take us to the end of March to reach the latitude of Paulet Island, and even then we cannot be certain of breaking out. Consequently my view is, 'Make as hard and as far as possible to the west.' The drift will take us north, and the resulting direction will be NW, the direction in which we want to go. . . . Anyway we will see what they think of things tomorrow."

7

Retreat

THE INSPECTION PARTY set out at
9 A.M., and the four men were back at
three o'clock, having gone a distance of some 6 miles.
Shackleton called all hands together at five o'clock and
informed them that "we could make progress to the west."
He said they would leave about thirty-six hours later,
very early on the morning of December 23, and they
would travel mostly at night when temperatures would
be lower and the ice surface firmer. They would take
only two boats, leaving the *Stancomb Wills* behind.

Furthermore, he said, since they would be on the trail
over Christmas, they would observe the holiday before
leaving and all hands could eat everything they wanted
for supper and the next day. A great deal of food would
have to be left behind anyway.

This last announcement was enough to win over all
but the stanchest holdouts against the plan. The Christmas "gorgie" began immediately and lasted almost all
the next day, with every man eating all he could hold—
"and everybody finishing up feeling full as a tick," Greenstreet remarked.

The men were called at three-thirty the following morning, and they started an hour later. By about 7 A.M.,

47

they had relayed the boats more than a mile to the west, and all hands went back to camp to eat breakfast. At nine o'clock, the teams were harnessed and set off toward the boats, pulling all the stores and equipment the sledges could carry. Shortly after 1 P.M., the tents were pitched at the new campsite and everybody turned in.

It was dismally wet. The tent floorings the men had devised at Ocean Camp had been left behind. Now they had only canvas ground covers or pieces of sail from the *Endurance,* which offered almost no resistance to the water covering the ice.

The men were roused for breakfast and the journey was resumed an hour later. But toward eleven o'clock, after they had made nearly a mile and a half, their way was blocked by a number of large cracks and bits of broken ice. The party pitched the tents at midnight and turned in. Most of the men were soaked through—from the water in which they lay, and from their own sweat. And none of them had a change of clothes except for socks and mittens, so they were forced to crawl into their sleeping bags wearing their soggy garments.

Shackleton went out with a three-man party early the following morning but could find no safe route for the boats. A long, dismal day was spent waiting to see what the ice might do. Just after supper they saw the ice begin to close, but it was not until 3 A.M. the next morning that they were able to get on the trail again.

The pitiful little line of march straggled across the floes in the pale half-light, with Shackleton in the lead, prospecting for the best route. Behind him were the seven sledges pulled by the dogs; then came a small sledge loaded with the blubber stove and cooking gear. It was pulled by Green and Orde-Lees, whose faces from being so close to the stove each day were black with blubber soot. At the rear of the column seventeen men under Worsley's command dragged the boats.

Even at 3 A.M., the coldest time of the day, the surface of the ice was treacherous. A crust had frozen over the rotting, saturated floes, and on top of this there was a layer of snow. Thus the surface had a deceptively sturdy appearance, and at each step it would seem capable of supporting a man. But just as he shifted his entire weight to that foot, he would burst through the crust with a jarring shock into the numbing water underneath. It was usually knee-deep, sometimes more.

Most of the men wore heavy boots designed for marching on hard ice. But as the party struggled over the slushy floes, those boots continually filled with water, and in the soaked state, each weighed about 7 pounds. It was an exhausting exertion at every step to lift one foot and then the other out of 2-foot holes full of snowy slush.

Of all the party, the worst off were the men pulling the boats. The shock they suffered at every step was greatly increased by their burden. They could take only about 200 to 300 yards of such punishment at a time. So they would abandon that boat and walk slowly back for the second, trying to catch their breath along the way. Frequently, they would find that the sledge runners under the second boat had frozen into the ice. There was nothing to do but slip into the traces, and then, with Worsley counting, "One, two, three . . . go!" they would make three or four violent, concerted lunges until the runners broke free.

At eight o'clock, after five hours on the trail, Shackleton signaled for a halt. They had covered half a mile. After an hour's rest, they struggled on until noon. The tents were pitched and supper was issued: cold seal steak and tea—nothing more.

On this same night exactly one year before, after a festive dinner on board the *Endurance*, Greenstreet had written in his diary: "Here endeth another Christmas Day. I wonder how and under what circumstances our next one will be spent." That night he failed even to mention what day it was. And Shackleton recorded briefly all that really needed to be said: "Curious Christmas. Thoughts of home."

The men were up at midnight, and resumed the march at 1 A.M. But at five o'clock, after four hours of all-out effort, the column stopped before a line of high pressure ridges and broad leads of water. While the rest of the party waited, Shackleton went out with Wild to look for a more passable route and found that beyond the area of pressure ridges there was a fairly level route. But it was decided to wait until night before pressing on.

All hands were turned out at eight o'clock that night, and after a hurried breakfast, the party set out once more. At first the going wasn't too bad, but shortly after midnight they came to an area of high pressure ridges which were so impassable that after two hours of exhausting

50

struggle they had covered less than a thousand yards. Yet still they kept at it, fighting to gain every foot of ground, until, bone weary, they pitched camp at six o'clock in the morning.

This travail of effort was resumed in the twilight of the evening after about nine hours of wet and troubled sleep. And though the condition of the ice seemed to get progressively worse, by 5:20 the next morning, the party had covered a gratifying two and a half miles.

Shackleton, however, was uneasy about the condition of the ice, and after camp had been pitched, he went with Hurley's team to survey what lay ahead. The two men reached a fragment of a berg and climbed it. The view from the top justified Shackleton's fears. He could see 2 miles ahead, and the ice was truly impassable—crisscrossed by leads of open water and the jumbled remains of broken pressure ridges. Moreover, it was dangerously thin. The two men returned to camp about seven o'clock and Shackleton reluctantly announced that they could not go any farther. Most of the men received the news with dismay. Not that they hadn't expected it, but to hear Shackleton himself say that they had been beaten sounded almost unnatural—and a little frightening.

None of them, however, could possibly have felt their defeat so intensely as Shackleton, to whom the thought of quitting was abhorrent. He wrote in his diary that night, with characteristically peculiar punctuation: "Turned in but could not sleep. Thought the whole matter over & decided to retreat to more secure ice: it is the only safe thing to do. . . . Am anxious: For so big a party & 2 boats in bad conditions we could do nothing: I do not like re-treating but prudence demands this course. . . ."

The retreat began at seven that night. They made their way back about a quarter mile to a fairly solid floe, and pitched camp. All hands were called early the next morning. Most of the men were sent out to hunt seals while Shackleton and Hurley prospected for a route to the northeast, and Worsley went with McIlroy's team to look for a way to the south. Neither party found a route that was safe.

Shackleton had noticed some breaking up of the ice around them. As soon as he returned to camp, he ordered the recall flag hoisted at once to summon the seal-hunting parties. Then once more the party retreated, this time about a half mile to a very flat, heavy floe. Even here they were not safe. A snow-filled crack was discovered in the ice the following morning, so they shifted camp about 150 yards toward the center of the floe in search of fairly stable ice. But there wasn't any to be found.

Worsley described the situation: "All the floes in the neighborhood appear to be saturated by the sea to the very surface, so much that on cutting 1 inch below the surface of a 6 or 7 feet thick floe, water almost at once flows into the hole."

But what disturbed them most was that they were trapped where they were. Greenstreet explained that "it looks as if we can get no further and we can't get back to Ocean Camp either as the floes have disintegrated con-siderably since we passed [over] them."

The following day was December 31. McNeish wrote:

"Hogmany [the Scottish feast of New Year's] & a bitter one too, being adrift on the ice instead of enjoying the pleasures of life like most people. But as the saying is, there must be some fools in this world."

James recorded: "New Year's Eve, the second in the pack & in much the same latitude. Few people are having a stranger one. . . ."

Macklin noted: "The last day of 1915 . . . tomorrow 1916 begins: I wonder what it will bring forth for us. This time last year we prophesied that just now we would be well across the Continent."

Finally, Shackleton wrote: "The last day of the old year: May the new one bring us good fortune, a safe deliverance from this anxious time & all good things to those we love so far away."

8

"Shoot the Dogs"

WORSLEY NAMED THE PLACE "Mark Time Camp," but it didn't seem an especially appropriate name. It implied that they had halted only temporarily, and would soon be on the move again. But nobody really believed they would.

After five days of exhausting struggle, they were suddenly idle. Now there was almost nothing to do, except to think. And there was altogether too much time for that.

Many of them, it seemed, finally grasped for the first time just how desperate things really were. More correctly, they became aware of their own inadequacy, of how utterly powerless they were. Until the march from Ocean Camp they had nurtured in the backs of their minds the attitude Shackleton strove so unceasingly to imbue them with, a basic faith in themselves—that they could, if need be, pit their strength and their determination against any obstacle—and somehow overcome it.

But then came the march, a journey which was to carry them nearly 200 miles. Yet after only five days and 9 small miles in a straight line to the northwest, they had been stopped completely, and even forced to retreat. A gale could easily have carried them that far in twenty-four hours. So now they sat in Mark Time Camp, disillusioned and humbly aware how truly pygmy they were to overcome the forces they faced, regardless of how much strength and determination they put forth. The realization was not so much humiliating as frightening.

Many of them made a sincere effort to be cheerful, but without much success. There was little to be cheerful about. The temperature remained just about at the freezing point, so that during the day the surface of the floes became a bog. They had to trudge about through knee-deep slush, and a man would often plunge up to his waist into an unsuspected hole. Their clothes were thus continually soaked, and their only comfort was crawling into the comparatively bearable dampness of their sleeping bags each night.

The food situation also was far from reassuring. There remained only fifty days' full trail provisions at 2 pounds per man—and the time when they would have looked upon such a supply as ample to see them out of the pack was long since past. They could hope to supplement their stores with seals and penguins, but there was disappointingly little game available—nowhere near as much as they had expected for this time of year. But on January 1, it seemed that the New Year might have brought with it a change of luck. Five crabeater seals and an emperor penguin were killed and brought into camp.

Returning from a hunting trip, Orde-Lees, traveling on skis across the rotting surface of the ice, had just about reached camp when an evil, knoblike head burst out of

55

the water just in front of him. He turned and fled, pushing as hard as he could with his ski poles and shouting for Wild to bring his rifle.

The animal—a sea leopard—sprang out of the water and came after him, bounding across the ice with the peculiar rocking-horse gait of a seal on land. The beast looked like a small dinosaur, with a long, serpentine neck.

After a half-dozen leaps, the sea leopard had almost caught up with Orde-Lees when it unaccountably wheeled and plunged again into the water. By then, Orde-Lees had nearly reached the opposite side of the floe; he was about to cross to safe ice when the sea leopard's head exploded out of the water directly ahead of him. The animal had tracked his shadow across the ice. It made a savage lunge for Orde-Lees with its mouth open, revealing an enormous array of sawlike teeth. Orde-Lees' shouts for help rose to screams and he turned and raced away from his attacker.

The animal leaped out of the water again in pursuit just as Wild arrived with his rifle. The sea leopard spotted Wild, and turned to attack him. Wild dropped to one knee and fired again and again at the onrushing beast. It was less than 30 feet away when it finally dropped.

Two dog teams were required to bring the carcass into camp. It measured 12 feet long, and they estimated its weight at about 1,100 pounds. It was a predatory species of seal, and resembled a leopard only in its spotted coat —and its disposition. When it was butchered, balls of hair 2 and 3 inches in diameter were found in its stomach

—the remains of crabeater seals it had eaten. The sea leopard's jawbone, which measured nearly 9 inches across, was given to Orde-Lees as a souvenir of his encounter.

In his diary that night, Worsley observed: "A man on foot in soft, deep snow and unarmed would not have a chance against such an animal as they almost bound along with a rearing, undulating motion at least five miles an hour. They attack without provocation, looking on man as a penguin or seal."

The hunting parties continued to operate the next day, though the warm, muggy weather kept the surface of the ice soggy. Four crabeater seals were secured and returned to camp. While they were being butchered, Orde-Lees came back from a trip on skis and announced that he had found and killed three more. But Shackleton contended that the party already had a month's supply, and ordered that the slain seals be left where they were.

Several men found Shackleton's attitude difficult to understand. Greenstreet wrote that he considered it "rather foolish . . . as things have not turned out at all as he had estimated up to the present, and it is far the best to be prepared for the possible chance of having to winter here."

Greenstreet was right. Like most of the others, he considered the laying in of all possible meat the prudent thing to do, as any ordinary individual might. But Shackleton was not an ordinary individual. He was a man who believed completely in his own invincibility, and to whom defeat was a reflection of personal inadequacy. What might have been an act of reasonable caution to the average person was to Shackleton a detestable admission that failure was a possibility.

This indomitable self-confidence of Shackleton's took the form of optimism. And it worked in two ways: it set men's souls on fire—as Macklin said, just to be in his presence was an experience.

But at the same time, the basic egotism that gave rise to his enormous self-reliance occasionally blinded him to realities. He tacitly expected those around him to reflect his own extreme optimism, and he could be almost petulant if they failed to do so. Such an attitude, he felt, cast doubt on him and his ability to lead them to safety.

Thus it was that the simple suggestion of bringing in three seals could be, to Shackleton's mind, an act of disloyalty. At another time he might have overlooked the incident. But just now he was hypersensitive. Almost everything he had undertaken—the expedition, saving the *Endurance,* and two attempted marches to safety— had failed miserably. In addition, the lives of twenty-seven other men were in his hands. "I am rather tired," he wrote one day. "I suppose it is the strain." Then later, "I long for some rest, free from thought."

For the next several days, living conditions seemed to deteriorate, if that was possible. The temperature climbed as high as 37 degrees, and the surface of the ice turned into pure slush. Food was growing short, and tempers shorter. Greenstreet wrote: "The monotony of life here is getting on our nerves. Nothing to do, nowhere to walk, no change in surroundings, food or anything. God send us open water soon or we shall go balmy."

Then on January 13, a rumor spread that Shackleton was considering killing the dogs to ease the drain on the food supplies. Among the men, reactions ranged from simple resignation to outraged shock. Stormy debates on the value of the dogs against the food they consumed broke out in each tent that night. But the fundamental, underlying factor in these discussions was that, for many men, the dogs were more than just so many pounds of pulling power on the trail; there was a deep emotional attachment involved. It was the basic human need to love something, the desire to express tenderness in this barren place. Though the dogs were vicious, surly beasts with one another, their devotion and loyalty toward the men was above question. And the men responded with an affection greatly surpassing anything they would have felt under ordinary conditions.

Under the best circumstances it would have been upsetting news. Under their present circumstances it was amplified in the minds of some men almost to a catastrophe. In their bitterness, a few, like Greenstreet, were inclined to fix the blame on Shackleton—with some justification: ". . . the present shortage of food," Greenstreet wrote, "is due simply and solely from the Boss refusing to get seals when they were to be had. . . . His sublime optimism all the way thro being to my mind absolute foolishness. Everything right away thro was going to turn out all right and no notice was taken of things possibly turning out otherwise and here we are."

But Shackleton made no mention of killing the dogs the next morning. Instead he ordered the men to shift camp because their floe was melting at a dangerous rate. The soot from the blubber stove had been tracked all over the surface of the ice, and it was holding the heat of the sun. The men began at noon to construct a roadway of blocks of ice and snow to bridge the gap to a floe about 150 yards to the southeast. The move was completed early in the afternoon. They named their new location "Patience Camp."

Then, in a quiet, level voice, Shackleton ordered Wild to shoot his own team along with McIlroy's, Marston's, and Crean's.

There was no protest, no argument. The four drivers obediently harnessed their teams and drove the dogs about a quarter of a mile away from the camp. The drivers then returned alone, except for McIlroy; he and Macklin were to assist Wild.

Each dog in turn was taken off his trace and led behind a row of large ice hummocks. There Wild sat the animal in the snow, took its muzzle in his left hand, and placed his revolver close to its head. Death was instantaneous.

After each dog had been killed Macklin and McIlroy dragged its body a short distance away, then returned to the waiting teams for the next animal. None of the dogs seemed to sense what was happening, and each went unsuspectingly around the ice hummock to his death with his tail wagging. When the job was done, the three men piled snow on top of the heap of dog bodies and walked slowly back to camp.

Shackleton decided to spare Greenstreet's team of year-old puppies "for the present," and he also granted a one-day reprieve to Hurley's and Macklin's teams so that they might be used to make a trip back to Ocean Camp for some of the food that had been left there.

The two sledges were made ready, and Hurley and Macklin started off at six-thirty that evening. It was an exhausting journey, lasting almost ten hours because they had to travel mostly over deep, soft snow and broken ice, and the dogs sank down to their bellies. However, at Ocean Camp, they managed to collect two loads of about 500 pounds apiece, consisting of canned vegetables, tapioca, dog pemmican, and jam. They prepared themselves a good meal of canned stew, fed the dogs, and started back at 6:30 A.M.

The return journey was comparatively easy because they had their own tracks to follow. The dogs pulled magnificently, though old Bos'n, Macklin's leader, was so exhausted he repeatedly vomited and staggered badly. The two sledges reached Patience Camp at one in the afternoon, and the dogs "dropped in the snow," Macklin recorded, "some of them not even rousing themselves to take their food."

Lying in his sleeping bag that night, Macklin wearily recorded the events of the journey in his diary. In a tired hand he concluded the entry: "My dogs will be shot tomorrow."

61

9

Hunger

TWO TENTS AWAY, old Chippy Mc-Neish was also writing his diary. It had been a discouraging day of muggy, dead-calm weather and the carpenter was tired. Since early morning he had been busy coating the seams of the boats with seal blood to keep the calking in once they were in the water. "No wind of any kind," he wrote. "We are still in hope of a sw breeze to relieve us before the winter sets in."

The next morning, three seals were sighted, and Macklin was sent out with Tom Crean to fetch them. When they returned, Shackleton told Macklin that since the party now had a fair supply of meat, his dogs would not be killed quite yet. But Hurley's team, including the leader, Shakespeare, the biggest of all the dogs, was shot. Wild, as usual, was executioner, and he took the dogs over to a distant floe to kill them. Macklin later found one of the dogs still alive, and immediately took out his knife and stabbed the animal to death.

About 3 P.M., the wind gently eased around to the southwest, and a chill came into the air. Throughout the night the temperature crept downward, and all the next day the southwest breeze held steady. That night Shackleton wrote, almost timorously, "This may be the turn in our fortune." By now the wind was not taken lightly. "It is spoken of with reverence," Hurley observed, "and wood must be touched when commenting thereon."

Somebody, it appeared, had touched the proper piece of wood. The wind came on the next day, a whole gale out of the southwest, with driving snow filling the air and the tents quaking with its violence. They huddled in their sleeping bags, dismally uncomfortable but radiantly happy. "Fifty miles an hour," McNeish recorded blissfully, "but it is welcome & as much more—as long as the tents stand." It howled on into January 19 unabated. Shackleton, the man of unbridled optimism, confined himself to guarded phrases lest he somehow hex this glorious wind. "We ought to be making North some now," he said with the utmost restraint.

On the twentieth, as the gale continued, a very few of them began to tire of the wet from the wind-driven snow filtering into the tents. "We are never satisfied," Hurley wrote, "as we are looking forward to a fine day. Our gear in the tents is becoming very wet and the opportunity of drying same will be hailed."

But most of them cheerfully endured the dreadful conditions, happy in the knowledge that they must be making good progress to the north.

"One hardly likes to guess what our distance may be," Shackleton wrote, more boldly, "but tonight is the fourth of this blow and there are no signs of it abating so we ought to have made a good distance to the North. Lees & Worsley are the only pessimistic ones in the camp but this strong wind even made Lees suggest larger steaks on the strength of our distance."

The next day the gale roared on, with a few gusts to 70 miles an hour. But twice during the morning the sun broke through the clouds. Worsley was ready with his sextant, and James stood by with his theodolite to catch the angle of the sun. They took their sights, worked out the calculations, and announced the result.

"Wonderful, amazing splendid," Shackleton wrote. "Lat. 65°43′ South—73 miles North drift. The most cheerful good fortune for a year for us: We cannot be much more than 170 miles from Paulet. Everyone greeted the news with cheers. The wind still continues. We may get another 10 miles out of it. Thank God. Drifting still all wet in the tents but no matter. Had bannock to celebrate North of the circle." The Antarctic Circle now lay nearly a full degree of latitude behind them.

The gale eased down the following day, and the sun shone brightly. Worsley got another sight which put their position at 65°32½′ South, 52°4′ West—11 miles north in twenty-four hours. It brought the total run since the beginning of the gale to 84 miles—in six days. Furthermore, the drift to the east, away from land, amounted to only a paltry 15 miles.

By evening the gale had blown itself out and the wind shifted to the north. But nobody minded. A northerly wind was just what they needed to open up the pack so that they could take to the boats. They waited . . . one day, two days, three days. But still the opening did not come, and Shackleton felt his patience growing thin. On January 30th, after a day of unrelieved monotony, he took his diary and wrote across the space provided for that day:

"Waiting
Waiting
Waiting."

But by the time a week had passed, most of the men were abandoning their hopes. They could see almost no change in the pack. If anything it was tighter than before, packed together by the force of the winds, and perhaps driven against some unknown land to the north or northwest. The sense of immediacy gradually diminished, and the atmosphere in camp settled once more into reluctant resignation.

Fortunately, the men were kept fairly well occupied hunting seals and sledging them into camp. On January 30, eight days after the gale ended, Shackleton decided to send Macklin and Crean on another trip to Ocean Camp with instructions to bring back anything of value they could find.

This time sledging conditions were considerably better and the trip took less than ten hours. The teams returned with some odds and ends of stores, including a quantity of canned herring, 60 pounds of bouillon cubes, and a large amount of tobacco. They also obtained a good number of books, among them several volumes of the *Encylopaedia Britannica,* which were especially welcome. Even McNeish, a devout Presbyterian, allowed as how he would enjoy a change from his Bible, which he had repeatedly reread from cover to cover.

For the next two days, Shackleton carefully observed the movements of the pack, and then he decided that a party of eighteen under Wild should start out early the next morning to bring up the *Stancomb Wills*. The news came as a great relief. For some time many of the men, particularly the seamen, had had strong misgivings about the advisability of trying to crowd the entire party into two boats.

"I am very glad," Worsley wrote. "If it comes to boats we shall be far safer in three; with only two it would be a practical impossibility to bring 28 men alive through a boat voyage of any length."

The sledging party was awakened at 1 A.M. the next morning, and after a good heavy breakfast they started off, dragging an empty boat sledge with them. It was an easy journey with so many men, and they arrived two hours and ten minutes later. Wild appointed Hurley cook, with James as his "mate and general hoosh stirrer." They put together a meal of anything they could find, and it wound up a mixture of dog pemmican, baked beans, and canned cauliflower and beets, cooked together in an empty gasoline can. Macklin pronounced it "very good," and James remarked with satisfaction that it was a "great success." The *Stancomb Wills* was safely back in Patience Camp by one o'clock.

Worsley wrote in his diary that night: "I was very

pleased that the Pack had kept solid long enough to bring our third boat across."

The trip to Ocean Camp changed the attitude of many men. Until then some vestige of anticipation that the pack might open had remained. But they had observed during the 12-mile round-trip journey to Ocean Camp that the ice was tighter than ever. The days of wishful thinking were over; there was nothing to do but sit down and wait.

Day after day after day dragged by in a gray, monotonous haze. The temperatures were high and the winds were light. Most of the men would have liked to sleep the time away, but there was a limit to the number of hours a man could spend inside his sleeping bag. Every available time-killing pastime was exploited to the fullest and often much beyond. On February 6, James wrote: "Hurley & Boss play religiously a set of six games of poker patience every afternoon. I think each rather regards it a duty but it certainly passes away an hour. The worst thing is having to kill time. It seems such a waste, yet there is nothing else to do."

Their most immediate concern just now was food. Early in February they had gone for almost two weeks without getting a seal, and while their meat supply was not yet too small, their stock of blubber for cooking was alarmingly low—only about enough for ten more days. On February 9, Shackleton wrote: "No seals. Must reduce blubber consumption . . . oh for a touch of dry land under our feet."

The following day, a party of men were set to digging into the snow-covered refuse heap to recover all possible blubber from the bones there. Seal flippers were cut up, and the decapitated heads of seals were skinned and scraped of every trace of blubber they afforded. But the amount obtained was insignificant, so Shackleton reduced their ration to one warm beverage a day—a serving of hot powdered milk at breakfast. The last of their cheese was served out the next day, and each man received a 1-inch cube. McNeish commented: "I smoked myself sick through trying to stifle the hunger this afternoon."

Then on the morning of February 17, as the blubber situation was becoming really desperate, somebody saw a flock of little Adélie penguins—about twenty altogether —sunning themselves a short distance from camp. A score of men seized any weapons that were handy—axe handles, picks, lengths of broken oars—and crept cautiously along almost on their hands and knees. When everybody was in position, the men rushed forward, clubbing furiously at the squawking, skittering Adélies. They killed seventeen in all. Other little bands were sighted throughout the day, and by nightfall they had brought in a total of sixty-nine penguins.

Despite the welcome addition to their larder, supper that night was frugal, consisting, McNeish noted, of "stewed penguin heart, liver, eyes, tongues, toes & God knows what else, with a cup of water" to wash it down. "I don't think any of us will have nightmares from overeating."

For the next two days, gale winds and heavy snow

68

forced the men to remain inside their tents. Yet all the while the croaking of Adélies continued, and when the weather finally cleared on February 20, thousands of penguins could be seen dotting the pack in every direction. They apparently were migrating north, and Patience Camp fortunately lay in the path of their trek.

All hands were put to the slaughter, bringing in every penguin that could be reached, and by evening they had killed 300. The following morning the men saw that the migration had moved on as suddenly as it had arrived, though for several days afterward, small bands of stragglers continued to appear, and by February 24 the party had secured a total of nearly 600. The Adélie, however, is a small and not very meaty bird, so that the amount of food obtained was not nearly so impressive as might be supposed. And the blubber on an Adélie is very small indeed.

Nevertheless, the sudden appearance of the penguins had removed, at least for the moment, the most serious threat they faced—starvation. And it was inevitable that their thoughts turned once more to their ultimate escape.

Greenstreet observed: "The food now is pretty well all meat. Seal steaks, stewed seal, penguin steaks, stewed penguin, penguin liver, the latter being very good indeed. The cocoa has been finished for some time and the tea is very nearly done and soon our only beverage will be [powdered] milk. Flour also is very nearly finished and is now used only with dog pemmican in the making of bannocks, which are damn fine. Our distance from Paulet I. is now 94 miles which means we have completed ¾ of the distance we had to do when we got on the floe. I wonder if we shall ever get there."

Macklin noted: "We have just been a third of a year on the floe, drifting as Nature has willed. I wonder when we shall see home again."

And James, ever the scientist, put it into laboratory terms: "We make all kinds of theories based sometimes on what we see about us of ice conditions, but more of this based on nothing at all. Can't help thinking of 'Theory of Relativity.' Anyhow we have only an horizon of a few miles & the Weddell Sea is roughly 200,000 sq. miles [actually it is closer to 900,000 square miles]. A bug on a single molecule of oxygen in a gale of wind would have about the same chance of predicting where he was likely to finish up."

10

A Promise Broken

I T HAD BEEN slightly more than a month since the end of the southerly gale. They had covered 68 miles, for an average daily drift of a little more than 2 miles. The over-all direction was northwest, but the day-by-day drift was an erratic, patternless movement, sometimes northwest, sometimes due west, even south, and, for a time, straight north. But they were definitely approaching the end of the Palmer Peninsula.

Worsley spent long, cold hours every day atop a small berg fragment looking anxiously to the west, hoping to sight land. On February 26, he saw "what may be Mount Haddington thrown up by refraction, 20 miles beyond its ordinary limits."

They wanted to believe it, but few of them did, least of all McNeish. "The skipper says he has seen it," he wrote, "but we know him to be a liar." Worsley was guilty of a bit of wishful thinking. Mount Haddington on James Ross Island lay more than 110 miles west of their position.

And so they drifted into March. On the fifth, Greenstreet wrote: "Day passes day with very little or nothing to relieve the monotony. We take constitutionals round and round the floe but no one can go further as we are to all intents and purposes on an island. There is practically nothing fresh to read and nothing to talk about, all topics being absolutely exhausted. . . . I never know what day of the week it is except when it is Sunday as we have Adélie liver and bacon for lunch and is the great meal of the week and soon I shall not be able to know Sunday as our bacon will soon be finished. The pack around looks very much as it did four or five months ago and with the low temperature we have been getting at night, i.e., zero and below, the open patches of water get covered with young ice which is neither fit to go over nor would allow the passage of the boats. My opinion is that the chances of getting to Paulet Is. now are about 1 in 10. . . ."

Indeed, the chances of reaching Paulet Island did appear more remote each day. It now lay exactly 91 miles away. But it was off to the WNW, and their drift had steadied onto a course almost true north. Unless there was a radical change in the northerly movement of the pack, it seemed that they would simply pass Paulet Island by. And there was nothing they could do about it, except to wait helplessly.

Then, on March 9, they felt the swell—the undeniable, unmistakable rise and fall of the ocean. There was no wishful thinking this time. It was there for all to see, and feel, and hear.

They noticed it first early in the morning as a strange, rhythmic creaking in the pack. The men gathered outside their tents and looked, and they could see it. The loose chunks of ice around the floe drew apart and closed again, 4 to 6 inches at a time. The large floes rose almost imperceptibly—not more than an inch—then, ever so slowly, fell again.

The men stood in excited little groups, pointing out to one another what was perfectly obvious to everyone—a gentle, lazy movement across the entire surface of the pack—the first outward sign of the proximity of the sea.

Long, speculative discussions were held all day as Worsley crouched by the edge of the floe and continued to time the infinitely slow rise and fall of the ice. By evening everyone was satisfied that the open ocean lay, at most, 30 miles away. Shackleton alone seemed to sense in the swell a new and far more grave threat than almost any they had faced. He wrote that night: "Trust will not increase until leads form."

He knew there could be no escape if the swells were to increase while the pack remained closed. The action of the sea would then crack and break the floes, ultimately grinding to bits the ice on which they could not camp, and through which they could not sail.

The men crawled out of their tents the next morning expecting to see that the swell had increased. Instead, there wasn't the slightest suggestion of movement in the pack, and the ice was as close as ever. A disappointment amounting to grief swept through most of the party. The first real sign of the open sea, the tantalizing promise of escape for which they had waited so long, had been dangled in front of them briefly—then snatched away.

That afternoon Shackleton ordered a drill to see how quickly the boats could be removed from their sledges and loaded with stores in case of an emergency. The men did what they had to do, but the raw edge of their tempers was beginning to show and there were a number of savage exchanges. Nor were matters improved when the stores were placed in the boats, and everybody could see for himself just how pitifully small their supplies really were. Certainly overloading was not going to be one of their problems. After the drill, the men returned moodily to their tents, hardly speaking to one another.

"Nothing to do, see or say," James recorded. "We find ourselves getting more taciturn daily."

11

"Land in Sight!"

To MAKE MATTERS WORSE, the problem of food—especially blubber for cooking—was again approaching the critical point. It was three weeks since they had killed a seal, and the meager store of blubber from the Adélies was almost gone. Their stock of provisions from the ship was also nearly exhausted. On March 16, the last of their flour was used up. It was made into dog pemmican bannocks, and several men nipped and nibbled at their 1-ounce portions for more than an hour.

And as the days went by their rations had to be decreased even more. The tea and coffee now were finished, and because of the shortage of blubber for fuel to melt ice into water, they were allowed only one ration of "very diluted" powdered milk a day. It was served at breakfast, along with five ounces of seal steak. Lunch was cold, a quarter can of frozen broth and one canned biscuit. Supper consisted of a serving of seal or penguin hoosh.

Most of the men felt the shortage of food almost as physical pain. The compulsive craving of their bodies for more fuel to burn to ward off the cold caused a gnawing, ceaseless hunger. And the weather was becoming

75

increasingly bitter, with nighttime temperatures frequently dropping as low as 10 below zero. Thus, when
their need for calories was greatest, they were forced to
get along on less than ever. Many men found that a few
hours after eating they had to crawl into their sleeping
bags to keep from shivering until the next meal put some
warmth back into them.

By March 22, the food situation was so critical that
Shackleton told Macklin that his dogs would have to be
shot the next day so that the party might eat the food set
aside for the dogs. Macklin reacted indifferently: "I must
confess that I cannot see that they will be of much more
use to us. Ocean Camp has apparently disappeared. We
have now only 10 more days blubber fuel—it is to be
hoped that we can get more seals, or we shall be in a bad
way indeed."

The morning of March 23 dawned cold, with a patchy
fog lying across the pack. Shackleton was up early and
he walked to the edge of the floe. Then the fog cleared
for a moment and he saw a black object far in the distance
to the southwest. He watched it for a few minutes, then
hurried back to his tent and roused Hurley. The two
men returned to the edge of the floe and peered for several minutes through the intermittent bands of fog.

It was there, all right—and it was land.

Shackleton immediately ran back to camp, going from
tent to tent shouting, "Land in sight! Land in sight!"
The reaction was strange. Some men bounded out of
their tents to see for themselves, but others—cold and
discouraged and tired of mistaking distant bergs for land

76

—refused to stir from their sleeping bags, at least until the sighting had been confirmed.

But this was not a distant berg or a mirage. It was one of the tiny Danger Islets, identifiable, according to the *British Antarctic Sailing Directions,* by its tabletop bluffs rising steeply out of the water. It lay exactly 42 miles away; and had the weather been good, it would have been possible to see Paulet Island, 20 miles beyond.

Early in the afternoon the weather cleared beautifully, revealing in the distance beyond the Danger Islets, the black base of a range of mountains, their peaks hidden in low-lying clouds. Worsley identified the tallest of the peaks as Mount Percy on Joinville Island off the very tip of the Palmer Peninsula.

The island lay just 57 miles very nearly due west of them—almost exactly at right angles to the direction of their drift. "If the ice opens we could land in a day," wrote Hurley.

But there wasn't a man among them who believed that the pack would open. Consequently, the sight of land was but another reminder of their helplessness. Greenstreet's attitude was rather typically cynical: "It is nice to think there is something else besides snow and ice in the world, but I fail to see any cause for excitement as it puts us no nearer getting out. What I would far rather see would be a crowd of seals coming up so that we might get food and fuel."

Yet frustrating as it was, the sight of land was welcome, as James noted, if for no other reason than "it is nearly 16 months since we last saw any black rock."

77

Macklin especially benefited since, in the excitement, Shackleton apparently forgot his decision to have Macklin's team killed.

"Please God," wrote Shackleton that night, "we will soon get ashore." But there was precious little land left on which to get ashore. They had drifted to the absolute tip of the Palmer Peninsula, and reaching land there now seemed all but impossible.

Thus, between them and the open seas and Cape Horn rollers of the dreaded Drake Passage—the most storm-torn ocean on the globe—all that remained were two lonely, sentinel-like outposts of the Antarctic Continent —Clarence and Elephant Islands, about 120 miles to the north. Beyond these, there was nothing.

Less than a week's supply of blubber remained, so on March 26 the 5-ounce ration of seal steaks at breakfast was cut out. In its place the men were usually given a half-pound cake of cold dog pemmican and a half-ration of powdered milk; on very cold days, a few lumps of sugar were added. Lunch was one biscuit and three lumps of sugar, and supper, the only so-called hot meal of the day, consisted of seal or penguin hoosh, "cooked for the minimum possible time." No water was issued at any time. If a man wanted a drink, he packed snow into a small can, usually a tobacco tin, and held it against his body to melt, or slept with it in his sleeping bag. But a full tobacco tin of snow yielded only a tablespoonful or two of water.

That afternoon Macklin was told to pick out anything

78

fit for human consumption from the stock of waste meat used to feed the dogs. Macklin sorted it out, setting aside everything "except that which was too stinking to contemplate eating." It was a repulsive collection of odd bits of flesh, Macklin noted, "and unfortunately, if we do not get more seals we will have to eat it raw."

It appeared, too, that the dogs would have to be eaten soon. They had been spared thus far because there was still a bare chance of making one last trip to Ocean Camp for the stores there. After that was done, or if it became evident that it could not be done, the dogs were to be shot and eaten.

"I would have no hesitation in eating dog cooked," wrote Macklin, "but I do not look forward to eating it raw."

For days, several men had strongly urged Shackleton to risk this one desperate dash back to Ocean Camp, now barely visible about 7 miles away. A 600- or 700-pound store of dog pemmican and about 60 pounds of flour still remained there. But Shackleton, though he was gravely concerned about the state of their supplies, could not bring himself to send the dog drivers across ice which was so obviously treacherous, and the trip to Ocean Camp was growing less feasible by the hour. Shackleton knew that it was now or never. Reluctantly he told Macklin that night to be ready for a possible start early the next morning. Macklin had already turned in, but he was so delighted at the news that he got up and worked for some time readying the harness and getting his sledge into shape. But at dawn the ice was very much on the move and a heavy mist had rolled in. Shackleton came to No. 5 tent just at breakfast time to inform Macklin that he had decided against the trip. It was a crushing disappointment, coming as it did on the heels of a miserable night of wet, misty weather, during which nobody had slept much.

Shackleton had hardly left, when, for some feeble reason, Macklin turned on Bobby Clark, the biologist, and the two men were almost immediately shouting at one another. The tension spread to Orde-Lees and Worsley and triggered a blasphemous exchange between them. In the midst of it, Greenstreet upset his powdered milk. He whirled on Clark, cursing him for causing the accident because Clark had called his attention for a moment. Clark tried to protest, but Greenstreet shouted him down.

Then Greenstreet paused to get his breath, and in that instant his anger was spent and he suddenly fell silent. Everyone else in the tent became quiet, too, and looked at Greenstreet, shaggy-haired, bearded, and filthy with blubber soot, holding his empty mug in his hand and looking helplessly down into the snow that had thirstily soaked up his precious milk. The loss was so tragic he seemed almost on the point of weeping.

Without speaking, Clark reached out and poured some of his milk into Greenstreet's mug. Then Worsley, then Macklin, and Rickenson and Kerr, Orde-Lees, and finally Blackboro. They finished in silence.

Later in the day, the misty weather turned to rain, then snow. James was night watchman that evening from nine to ten, and as he was walking around the floe, he thought he detected a movement in the ice. Looking closely, he saw a "very distinct swell" slowly lifting the floe. He reported his discovery to Shackleton, who gave orders that the watchman should be especially alert.

At five-twenty the next morning the floe split.

12

"Launch the Boats!"

LITTLE ALF CHEETHAM was on watch, and he dashed among the tents.

"Crack!" he shouted. "Crack! Lash up and stow!"

Within seconds, all hands had tumbled out of their tents. They saw two cracks, one running the length of the floe and another extending at right angles to the first. In addition, the whole pack was rising to a very marked swell.

They ran to the *James Caird* and wrenched the frozen runners of her sledge free of the ice, then manhandled her to the center of the floe. By then the crack down the center had widened out to 20 feet in some places, and could be seen slowly working back and forth under the influence of the swell. Their store of meat was on the other side. Several men jumped across where the crack was not so wide and pitched the meat over the seam of open water.

By 6:45, everything was safely across and work was halted for breakfast. The men were standing around waiting for their ration when the floe cracked again, this time directly under the *James Caird*, 100 feet from the tents. No order was needed. The men dashed to the boat and quickly brought her up closer to the tent area. Finally, they were able to eat breakfast—the usual lump of dog pemmican, six pieces of sugar, and a half-mug of milk.

Breakfast was hardly finished when through the mists, a strange shape appeared, moving deliberately across a nearby section of their old floe. Wild ran to get his rifle from his tent, then he dropped to one knee and shot. The animal bucked, and slowly sank down onto the ice. Several men hurried to where it lay—a sea leopard nearly 11 feet long.

With one bullet, it seemed, Wild had changed the whole complexion of their lives. There at their feet lay nearly 1,000 pounds of meat—and at least two weeks' supply of blubber. Shackleton announced that they would feast on the sea leopard's liver for lunch.

In high good spirits, the party sent out the dogs to return the trophy to camp. When it was butchered, they found in its stomach nearly fifty undigested fish, which were carefully set aside to be eaten the next day. It was nine o'clock by the time the job was finished.

Shackleton then summoned Macklin and told him the time had come to shoot his dogs. Macklin made no protest, for there was really no longer any reason to spare them. The possibility of reaching Ocean Camp was more remote than ever in view of the new breakup, and now that they had the sea leopard, the need for risking such a trip was past.

Accompanied by Wild, Macklin drove his team across the narrow neck of a crack to where the galley formerly had stood. On the way, they passed what had been the meat dump. Songster, a wily old dog, grabbed up a discarded penguin head, and Bos'n got hold of a bone. They were both allowed to keep them.

Macklin was almost sick as he unharnessed one dog at a time and took it around the protective mound of ice. Wild, as before, sat each dog down in the snow, placed the muzzle of the revolver almost against its head, and pulled the trigger. Songster died with the penguin head in his mouth, and Bos'n died gripping his bone. When all the dogs had been killed, Macklin skinned and gutted the carcasses, preparing them for eating. Crean's team of puppies was also killed and butchered.

Back at camp, there was almost a holiday atmosphere in anticipation of the first hot lunch in more than two weeks. The suggestion was made that they sample the dog meat, and Shackleton agreed. Crean cut small steaks from his dog, Nelson, and Macklin did the same with Grus.

When the meat had been fried, Crean hurried around to distribute it. He went first to Shackleton's tent, poking his weathered, Irish face through the flap. "I've just brought a bit of Nelson for you to try," he said puckishly.

The meat of the dogs was universally acclaimed. "Their flesh tastes a treat," McNeish remarked. "It is a big treat to us after being so long on seal meat." James found it "surprisingly good and tasty." Worsley said that the piece of Grus he ate "has a better flavor than the sea leopard." And Hurley went so far as to say it was "exquisitely tender and flavorous, especially Nelson, which equaled veal."

Throughout the morning the swell had continued and even increased slightly, so at lunch Shackleton announced that a system of patrols would begin immediately.

During the day, there were more and more signs of an imminent opening. Cape pigeons and terns could be seen overhead, and Worsley sighted a magnificent giant petrel, snow white except for two bands of black across its wings—a definite sign of open water. These, plus a black water sky to the northwest, the presence of the swell, and a high temperature of 34 degrees, led Worsley to remark: "It certainly looks promising." But then he added: "Hope tells a flattering tale."

In spite of all the encouraging signs, the pack showed little change throughout the day and into the next morning; though in the afternoon a very dark water sky appeared in the southwest, stretching all the way around to the northeast.

That evening, just at eight o'clock as Macklin was relieving Orde-Lees on watch outside, the floe unexpectedly rose to a swell and cracked, hardly 2 feet from Wild's tent. Macklin and Orde-Lees both spread the alarm.

Everybody had turned in, confident that there would be no breakup, and the emergency caught them almost totally unprepared. There was a great scramble to get dressed in the pitch-black tents, with everyone trying to find the right clothes and attempting to get into boots that had frozen in the 20-degree cold. But order was finally restored; the boats were moved closer to the tents, and the stock of meat, which again had been cut off by a crack, was pitched across in the darkness.

Shackleton ordered that full sea watches be set, and that the off-duty men turn in "all standing"—fully dressed, including mittens and helmets.

It was hard to sleep. Throughout the night the floe lifted very noticeably to the heavy swell, perhaps a foot or more, and the repeated shocks as it bumped against other floes were disconcerting. The men all knew that the floe was now so small that should it crack again, something—or somebody—would almost inevitably fall through and probably be crushed.

But when morning came the southerly wind dropped, and during the forenoon the swell disappeared. At noon, for the first time in six days, Worsley obtained a sight. It put their position at 62°33′ South, 53°37′ West. They had drifted an astonishing 28 miles north in six days, and this in spite of five days of adverse northerly winds. The pack was obviously under the influence of a northerly current.

And so a new menace had been introduced: if the pack were to be swept rapidly northward, and yet remain too close to launch the boats, it would mean simply that they were doomed. They would then be carried beyond Clarence and Elephant Islands into the open sea, and once there, the ice would unquestionably be dissipated, leaving them at best adrift in the boats, exposed to the full fury of the storms in the Drake Passage. "God forbid we should get that," wrote Greenstreet, "for I doubt if we would survive."

James recorded: "A great air of expectancy everywhere. We are on the verge of something, there is no doubt. . . . Our chief need is an opening in the ice. Our chief danger being carried beyond these islands in close pack."

And so the watch had begun. It was April 3, and every day, almost every hour, the situation changed, growing ever more desperate.

On April 5, Worsley obtained a position which showed unmistakably that their fears of being blown out to sea were altogether justified. But then at daybreak the following morning, a huge berg was sighted almost due north. Only it wasn't a berg—it was Clarence Island, and more important, its bearing showed that their seaward drift had been arrested, and the pack was still on course—though tight as ever.

"Pray God we may find a landing here," wrote Macklin, "and so be off this drifting uncontrollable pack, taking us we know not where. . . ."

About 6:45 the next evening, McNeish was writing in his diary. "There has been a large swell since yesterday," he recorded. "But it is doing us no harm now because our floe is broken up so small. It rises and falls with. . . ." He never finished the sentence.

There was a jarring shock, and the floe split once more. By the time the stores and boats had been repositioned, Patience Camp was a triangle of ice whose sides measured roughly 100 × 120 × 90 yards.

Not long after midnight, great pools of open water ap-

87

peared as the floes drew apart. But by daybreak the ice had closed again, though the sky to the north grew black as ink. Again at breakfast the ice mysteriously moved apart, but once more it was only temporary. Toward mid-morning, for the third time, large pools of open water unaccountably spread through the pack and widened out. Shackleton's booming brogue rang out: "Strike the tents and clear the boats!"

Crack!

Again the floe had split in two, this time exactly through the spot where Shackleton's tent had stood some minutes before. The men looked at Shackleton.

For the moment the pack was open—but how long would it remain open? And yet, how long could they stay where they were? The immense floe that had once been Patience Camp was now an irregular rectangle of ice hardly 50 yards across. How long would it be before it was broken and ground to bits beneath their feet?

At twelve-forty, Shackleton gave the order in a quiet voice.

"Launch the boats."

The floe came alive with activity. Green ran to his stove and put out the fire. Other men took pieces of canvas and tied up small piles of meat and blubber. The rest of the party hurried to the boats.

The *Dudley Docker* was removed from its sledge and eased into the water. Then with all hands passing stores, she was loaded with cases of rations, a bag of meat, the blubber stove, and No. 5's rattly old hoop tent. An empty sledge was lowered into the water and tied onto

88

her stern. Next the *Stancomb Wills* was rapidly launched and loaded, and finally the *James Caird*.

It was one-thirty in the afternoon when the crews scrambled on board each boat; they put out every available oar and pulled with all their strength for the open water.

Even as they drew away from Patience Camp, the ice began to close.

13

Escape to Danger

THE FIRST FEW MINUTES WERE crucial—and they were maddening. The oarsmen did their best to pull together, but they were clumsy and out of practice, and hampered by their own anxiety. The encircling ice fouled the oars, and collisions were unavoidable. Men crouched in the bows of each boat and tried to pole off the bigger pieces of ice, but a great many outweighed the boats themselves.

The raised sides of the *James Caird* and the *Dudley Docker* were an added hindrance. They made the seats too low for proper rowing, and though cases of stores were placed under the four oarsmen in each boat, it was still an awkward business.

The sledge astern of the *Dudley Docker* continually got hung up on bits of ice, and after a few minutes Worsley angrily cut it loose.

And yet, to their surprise and almost in spite of themselves and the jealous hands that tried to hold them back, they were making headway. With each boat-length the ice seemed looser. It was difficult to tell whether the pack was opening or whether they were escaping from the ice surrounding Patience Camp. In either case, for the moment, luck was on their side.

The overcast sky seemed almost alive with birds—Cape pigeons, terns, fulmars, and Antarctic, silver-gray and snow petrels by the thousands. The birds were so thick their droppings spattered on the boats and forced the rowers to keep their heads lowered. Whales, too, seemed everywhere. They surfaced on all sides, sometimes frighteningly close—especially the killers.

The *James Caird* was in the lead with Shackleton at the tiller. So far as the ice permitted he set a course for the northwest. Next came Worsley steering the *Dudley Docker,* then Hudson in the *Stancomb Wills.* The sound of their voices chanting, "stroke ... stroke ... stroke ..." mingled with the cries of the birds overhead and the surge of the swell through the pack. With each stroke, the oarsmen fell more into the rhythm of their task.

In fifteen minutes, Patience Camp was lost in the confusion of ice astern. But Patience Camp no longer mattered. That soot-blackened floe which had been their prison for nearly four months—whose every feature they knew so well, as convicts know each crevice of their cells; which they had come to despise, but whose preservation they had prayed for so often—belonged now to the past. They were in the boats ... actually in the boats, and that was all that mattered. They thought neither of Patience Camp nor of an hour hence. There was only the present, and that meant row ... get away ... escape.

Within thirty minutes they had entered an area of very open pack, and by two-thirty they were easily a mile away from Patience Camp.

The position when the boats were launched was 61° 56' South, 53°56' West, near the eastern reaches of what is called Bransfield Strait, a body of water about 200 miles long and 60 miles wide, lying between the Palmer Peninsula and the South Shetland Islands. It connects the hazardous Drake Passage with the waters of the Weddell Sea. Even today, the U.S. Navy Department's *Sailing Directions for Antarctica,* in describing conditions in Bransfield Strait, frankly admits the scarcity of information about the area. "It is believed," the *Sailing Directions* continue, that strong, erratic currents are to be found, sometimes reaching a velocity of 6 knots. These currents are affected only slightly by the wind, so that often a condition known to sailors as a "cross sea" is set up—when the wind is blowing in one direction, and the current moving in another. At such times, angry hunks of water—3, 6, 10 feet high—are heaved upwards, much as when breakers are thrown back from a bulkhead and collide with incoming waves. A cross sea is a perilous thing to a small boat.

Furthermore, the weather in Bransfield Strait is reliably inhospitable. Snows are heavy and gales are common, beginning in the middle of February and becoming more frequent and more violent as the Antarctic winter draws closer.

The boats in which the party set sail upon this forbidding sea were sturdy enough, but no open boat was really equal to the voyage they faced. The *Dudley Docker* and the *Stancomb Wills* were cutters—heavy, square-sterned boats of solid oak, 21 feet 9 inches long, with a 6-foot-2-inch beam, and they had three seats, or thwarts, plus a small decking in the bow and in the stern. They also mounted stubby masts to which a sail could be secured; but they were primarily pulling boats, designed for rowing, not sailing. The only real difference between the two was that McNeish had added planks to the *Dudley Docker,* which raised her sides about 8 inches.

The *James Caird* was a double-ended whaleboat, 22 feet 6 inches long and 6 feet 3 inches wide. Though she was somewhat larger than the other two, she was a lighter, springier boat. McNeish had raised her sides about 15 inches, and she was thus by far the most seaworthy of the three.

In terms of weight, the boats were not overloaded. The *Wills* carried eight men, the *Docker* nine and the *Caird* eleven; in less stormy waters, with less bulky gear, each might have accommodated at least twice that number. As matters stood, the boats were uncomfortably crowded. The hoop tents and the rolled-up sleeping bags took up a disproportionate amount of room. There were also cases of stores and a considerable amount of personal gear—all of which left scarcely enough space for the men themselves.

Throughout the afternoon, as they held to a north-westerly course, the three boats made excellent progress. There were belts of ice that were fairly thick, but none so dense as to block their way. Shortly after five o'clock the light began to fail. Shackleton called to the other boats to stay close by until a suitable camping place was

93

found. They rowed until about five-thirty when they came to a flat, heavy floe some 200 yards across, which Shackleton decided was sturdy enough to camp on. Green set up his blubber stove while the remainder of the party pitched the tents. Supper consisted of a quarter-pound of dog pemmican and two biscuits apiece. It was finished by eight o'clock, and all hands except the watch turned in. It had been a tiring but exciting day. By Worsley's estimate, they had made a good 7 miles to the northwest. Though the distance itself was not impressive, the fact that they had finally taken to the boats was the fulfillment of a dream. After five and a half months on the ice, they were underway at last, "doing some good for oneself," as Macklin put it. They dropped off to sleep almost immediately.

Toward eleven o'clock, Shackleton became strangely uneasy, so he dressed and went outside. He noticed that the swell had increased and their floe had swung around so that it was meeting the seas head on. He had stood watching for only a few moments, when there was a deep-throated thud and the floe split beneath his feet—and directly under No. 4 tent in which the eight forecastle hands were sleeping.

Almost instantly the two pieces of the floe drew apart, the tent collapsed and there was a splash. The crewmen scrambled out from under the limp canvas.

"Somebody's missing," one man shouted. Shackleton rushed forward and began to tear the tent away. In the dark he could hear muffled, gasping noises coming from below. When he finally got the tent out of the way, he saw a shapeless form wriggling in the water—a man in his sleeping bag. Shackleton reached down for the bag and with one tremendous heave, he pulled it out of the water. A moment later, the two halves of the broken floe came together with a violent shock.

The man in the sleeping bag turned out to be Ernie Holness, one of the firemen. He was soaked through but he was alive, and there was no time to worry about him then because the crack was opening once more, this time very rapidly, cutting off the occupants of Shackleton's tent and the men who had been sleeping in the *Caird* from the rest of the party. A line was pitched across and the two little groups of men, pulling toward one another, managed to bring the halves together once more. The *Caird* was hurriedly shoved across and then the men leaped to the larger floe. Shackleton waited until the others were safe, but by the time it was his turn, the pieces had drifted apart again. He took hold of the rope and tried to bring his chunk closer; however, with only one man pulling it was useless. Within ninety seconds he had disappeared into the darkness.

For what seemed a very long interval, no one spoke; then from the darkness they heard Shackleton's voice. "Launch a boat," he called.

Wild had just given the order. The *Wills* was slid into the water, and a half-dozen volunteers scrambled on board. They put out their oars and rowed towards Shackleton's voice. Finally they saw his outline in the

95

darkness, and they pulled up alongside his floe. He jumped into the *Wills,* and they returned to the campsite.

Sleep now was out of the question. Shackleton ordered the blubber stove lighted. Then he turned his attention to Holness, who was shivering uncontrollably in his soaked clothes. But there weren't any dry garments to give him because their only clothes were the ones they were wearing. To prevent Holness from freezing, Shackleton ordered that he be kept moving until his own clothes dried. For the rest of the night, the men took turns walking up and down with him. His companions could hear the crackling of his frozen garments, and the tinkle of the ice crystals that fell from him. Though he made no complaint about his clothes, Holness grumbled for hours over the fact that he had lost his tobacco in the water.

14

A Dream Destroyed

AT 5 A.M., the first hint of a brightening sky marked the ending of the night. It was April 10.

The weather at daybreak was hardly encouraging—overcast and hazy. Neither Clarence nor Elephant Island was visible, and Worsley could only estimate that they lay generally to the north, between 30 and 40 miles away. At eight-ten Shackleton gave the order to launch the boats.

The sea was broken by a nasty chop which made the boats lurch heavily, and rowing extremely difficult. But before long the ice began to open up, and within an hour or so they found themselves in a vast expanse of ice-free water, so broad they could hardly see the pack to either side. It was a welcome sight after more than a year of looking at nothing but ice. Shackleton had the word passed to hoist sail.

The *Caird* was fitted with two masts for a mainsail and a mizzen, plus a small jib in the bow. The *Docker* carried a single lug sail, and the *Wills* mounted only a very small mainsail and jib. The boats were thus hardly fit sailing companions—and this fact immediately became apparent when the sails were set. The *Caird* caught the wind and heeled to port, drawing steadily ahead of the other two boats. Though the *Docker* was somewhat faster than the *Wills,* the difference was slight, and neither boat could sail into the wind. There was nothing for the *Caird* to do but to hang back so as not to outdistance the others.

Toward midmorning the boats came to a boundary of pack ice stretching in a long, closely packed line, apparently following the current. For more than an hour, the three boats proceeded west along its edge, but then, shortly after eleven o'clock, a passage was discovered and the men rowed through.

They realized immediately that they must be in the open ocean. Ironically, here was the moment they had dreamed of ever since the days at Ocean Camp—but the reality was vastly different from the dream. As soon as the boats emerged from the protective barrier of the pack, they were struck by the full force of the wind, and a high, breaking sea was running down from the northeast. Freezing spray burst over them as they tried to beat their way to the NNE under sail. Time after time, icy blasts whipped them across the face, and the penetrating wind seemed all the colder because of their lack of sleep. In the *Docker,* Orde-Lees and Kerr slumped down onto the pile of sleeping bags, miserably seasick.

Yet the men complained very little. They knew that somewhere through the mists, probably not more than two dozen miles to the north, there was land, and they were actually making for it, and getting closer all the time. When it came time for lunch, Shackleton permitted a hearty ration of biscuits, cold sledging ration, dog pemmican, and six lumps of sugar.

Early in the afternoon, however, the wind increased considerably, and the boats began to take on water at a dangerous rate. Toward two o'clock, Shackleton realized that it was foolhardy to press on, and ordered them back behind the protective line of the pack.

The boats came about and sped southward before the following wind. Within minutes they had reached the edge of the pack, and they proceeded westward, looking for a floe to which they might make fast. The largest single piece of ice they could find was what Worsley described as a "floe-berg," a thick mass of dark blue pressure ice about 35 yards square, which rose in some places to a height of 15 feet above the water. It was floating alone, isolated from the rest of the line of pack, and it had obviously been adrift for a long time. The seas had eaten around its waterline, leaving an overhanging girdle of rotten ice.

The perils of the sleepless night before were still altogether too vivid in Shackleton's memory to risk again. The party would have to spend the night in the boats. They pulled up alongside the floe-berg, and drove oars into the ice. Then they made the bow lines of the boats fast to the oars, and the boats lay off to wait for darkness.

Within minutes, however, the wind freshened out of the northeast, and the sea picked up. The boats began to bump heavily, and they threatened to uproot the oars which held them to the floe. The wind swirled across the surface of the berg, catching snow from its surface and hurling it straight into the men's faces. After about a half hour of this misery, Shackleton had no choice. If the men were to sleep—and they had to sleep—there was no alternative to camping on the ice. Reluctantly he gave the order.

The boats were maneuvered alongside the floe-berg and about half the party scrambled onto the ice. The stores and equipment were quickly passed up. Then came the ordeal with the boats. The rotten overhang around the edge of the floe-berg made it necessary to haul the boats almost straight up while the men pulled from a safe distance back from the edge.

It was three-thirty before everything was safe, and by then the men were very nearly exhausted. They had hardly slept for thirty-six hours. Their hands, unaccustomed to rowing, were blistered and a little frostbitten. Their clothes were soaked from the spray in the boats, and when they unrolled their sleeping bags they found them wet through.

But all that mattered then was sleep. After a supper of cold dog pemmican, milk, and two lumps of sugar, they wriggled, fully dressed, into their sleeping bags. A few men, before they closed their eyes, put forth one last bit of effort to record the day's events briefly in their diaries. Worsley wrote: "By my reckoning we make today [northwest] 10 miles, and the current should run us well to the West before this strong Easterly breeze." And Hurley recorded the one thought that was uppermost in all their minds: ". . . pray God [this floe] will remain entire throughout the night."

By some minor miracle it did, but long before dawn they became aware that something was seriously wrong. At sunrise, they awakened to a terrifying spectacle of nature.

During the night, the wind had risen almost to gale force, and from somewhere to the northeast, great quantities of pack had drifted down on them. Now it extended unbroken to the horizon in every direction. Berg fragments and shattered floes in ten-thousand different shapes obliterated the surface of the water. And out of the northwest, rollers 30 feet high, stretching from horizon to horizon, swept down through the pack in long, implacable lines a half mile apart. At their summits the floe-berg was lifted to what seemed like dizzying heights, then dropped into valleys from which the horizon was obscured. The air was filled with a dull, muddled roar —the low shriek of the wind, and the seas breaking hoarsely amongst the pack, along with the incessant booming grind of the ice.

Because of its size, their berg was drifting more slowly than the rest of the pack, which bore down upon it and pounded it on every side, while the surge of the swell was undermining it by eating away at the waterline. Periodically, decayed chunks dropped away from one side or another, and others were torn loose by floe fragments hurled against the berg by the seas. At each impact, the berg shuddered sickeningly.

This was precisely the situation Shackleton had feared since the first appearance of the swell at Patience Camp. The berg was crumbling beneath them, and might split or upend at any moment. And yet to launch the boats would have been idiocy. They would have been splintered to bits in ninety seconds.

The whole scene had a kind of horrifying fascination. And watching it, many of the men sought to put their feeling into words. But they could find no words that were adequate. The lines in Tennyson's *Morte d'Arthur* kept running through Macklin's head: ". . . I never saw, nor shall see, here or elsewhere, till I die, not though I live three lives of mortal men, so great a miracle. . . ."

Shackleton climbed to a knoll a dozen feet high at one end of the berg from which he could see the limitless expanse of ice. Here and there, far away, a black line or a small dark patch revealed a lead or a pool of open water. The party's only hope was that one of these openings would drift down and surround the berg, making possible their escape. But time and time again, a lead would approach to within a short distance, then veer to one side or another or vanish altogether as the ice closed up. Hour after hour they waited—eight, nine, ten o'clock. Since dawn the boats had been ready, and the stores and equipment lay close by for immediate loading.

Occasionally Shackleton would call to the men to stand by. A chance was coming. They would rush to the boats and wait, but after a time Shackleton would look down and shake his head. The chance was gone.

While they waited, the berg was being systematically destroyed, piece by piece. Late in the morning, a huge sea burst against it, and a 20-foot section slipped into the water.

Noon came. The berg was smaller, but the ice was just as close. If anything, the swell was higher. Some sledging ration was issued and the men ate standing in little groups, talking quietly. By one o'clock, a sickening thought had begun to spread through the party. What if darkness came and the ice was still tight? With the beating it was taking, the berg could not possibly last until the next morning. They would be pitched into the sea during the night.

The men made feeble jokes about it, tried to resign themselves, or simply tried not to think about it. Greenstreet took his diary and attempted to write: "... a very anxious time as our floe was rocking and rolling heavily being...." The diary ended there in midsentence. It was no good; he couldn't keep his mind on it.

Shortly before two o'clock, when only about three hours of daylight remained, a somber quiet came over the party. Lead after lead had drifted past, too far away to do them any good. They were watching Shackleton as he followed still another lead approaching from the north, but no one thought it would really be their chance.

There was an excited shout. A pool was opening in the opposite direction. They turned and stared. What they saw was almost beyond belief. The ice was mysteriously drawing away, as if under the influence of some invisible force. As they looked, eddies and swirls riffled the surface of the water. A freak current had apparently risen from the depths of the sea and been deflected against the deep underside of the berg. They jumped up and down, pointing and gesturing wildly toward the pool of inky water that was widening out from the berg.

"Launch the boats," Shackleton cried as he raced down from his perch. "Chuck in the stores any old way." Anxious hands seized the boats and hurried them to the edge of the berg. The surface of the sea was 5 feet beneath them, so the men almost pitched the boats off the ice into the water. Crewmen dropped into them and the stores were hurried on board. In five minutes the boats were away.

They pulled to the center of the pool, and from there they could see still another pool beyond a narrow neck of brash ice. They pushed through the ice, and then the pack, in its inexplicable way, began to dissipate, leaving an ample margin of open water around them.

Until now, the destination had been either Clarence or Elephant Island—whichever the party happened to strike. These were the most logical choices, the closest bits of land. At the time the boats were launched from Patience Camp, Clarence Island lay just 39 miles almost due north. By sailing northwest, they had reduced that distance to about 25 miles NNE, Worsley estimated. However, it had been two days since the last observation, and during that time the strong winds out of the northeast had probably blown the party a considerable distance to the west. Furthermore, the greatest quantities of open water now extended to the southwest—toward King George Island, 80-odd miles away. Shackleton made the decision on the spot: they would abandon the effort to reach Clarence or Elephant Island and take advantage of the following wind to make for King George Island.

They held to a southwest course throughout the afternoon. About three-thirty, Shackleton signaled from the *Caird* to hoist sail, and almost immediately, the inequalities in the three boats became apparent once more. The *Caird* clove neatly through the water, followed by the *Docker,* but the *Wills* limped along astern, dropping farther back all the while. After a time, Shackleton brought the *Caird* up under the lee of some ice and shouted to Worsley to go back after the *Wills.* It took almost an hour for the *Docker* to beat her way to windward, take the *Wills* in tow, and return to the *Caird.*

By the time the three boats were joined up once more, darkness was rapidly approaching, and Shackleton was afraid of a collision with the ice. The boats took in their sails and proceeded under oars. In the last glimmer of light, they found a floe and drew alongside it. But there was to be no camping this night—nor ever again, so far as Shackleton was concerned. They had learned their lesson twice over, and they were through with the ice for good. The only man to debark now was Green, who carried his blubber stove and supplies onto the floe. He brewed up some seal hoosh and warmed some milk. The men ate sitting in the boats.

When they had finished, they cast off. The boats were made fast, one behind the other, with the *Docker* in the lead. Then the party began to row, very slowly, toward the southwest. They took spells at the oars, two men pulling at a time. Others hunched in the bows of the boats as lookouts, watching for the edge of the pack so that the boats might stay behind its protective line, and keeping an eye out for bergs or large floes that might catch and crush the boats. It had begun to snow—large, wet flakes that clung and melted. The snow doubled the discomfort of the lookouts, straining their eyes into the wind to watch for ice drifting down out of the darkness.

The period at the oars was kept short so that each man had a turn as often as possible. It was the only way to keep warm. Those who were not rowing or on lookout did what they could to keep their blood moving. But sleep was out of the question, for there was nowhere to lie down. The bottom of each boat was so packed with stores that there was scarcely room for the men's feet. Sleeping bags and tents took up most of the space in the bows, and the two thwarts on which the oarsmen sat had to be kept free. That left only a small space midships for the off-duty men to sit in a tight little group, huddled together for warmth.

Throughout the night, the sudden eruption of water nearby and a sound like a steam valve popping under pressure told of whales blowing close at hand. They became the primary worry during that long, black night. Whales had been seen on hundreds of occasions tossing aside vast chunks of floes as they surfaced to breathe. And the ability of a whale to discriminate between the underside of a floe and the white bottoms of the boats was open to serious question.

About 3 A.M., the entire party was suddenly electrified

by an almost hysterical shout from Hudson. "A light! A light!" He was pointing to the northwest. Every man sat upright, staring off in the direction Hudson indicated. The excitement lasted for only one cruel moment—until they were alert enough to realize the absurdity of it. Then they settled down again, cursing Hudson for his stupidity and for having raised their hopes. But Hudson insisted that he had seen it, and for several minutes he sat disconsolately mumbling to himself because nobody would believe him.

Toward five o'clock, the sky began to brighten. Before long the dawn of April 12 broke in radiant splendor along the horizon. The sun started its climb into a cloudless sky, and the mere sight of it seemed to change the whole shape of things. They rowed alongside a large floe, and Green again jumped ashore to prepare some seal hoosh and hot milk. After breakfast they cast off and set sail to the southwest under perfect conditions—wide stretches of open water protected by a line of pack on which hundreds of seals lay sleeping.

About ten-thirty, Worsley took out his sextant. Then, bracing himself against the mast of the *Docker*, he carefully took his sight—the first since leaving Patience Camp. At noon he repeated the procedure, as the boats lay to awaiting the result. Every face was turned toward Worsley as he sat in the bottom of the *Docker* working out his figures. They watched to see his expression when the two lines of position were plotted for a fix. It took him much longer than usual, and gradually a puzzled look came over his face. He checked his calculations

107

over, and the expression of puzzlement gave way to one of worry. Once more he ran through his computations; then he slowly raised his head. Shackleton had brought the *Caird* alongside the *Docker,* and Worsley showed him the position—62° 15' South, 53° 7' West.

They were 124 miles nearly due east of King George Island and 61 miles southeast of Clarence Island—22 miles farther from land than when they had launched the boats from Patience Camp three days before!

15

"All, All Alone . . ."

THEY HAD CONTINUALLY SAILED WEST, with strong easterly winds driving them along—and yet they had actually been going in the opposite direction. They were 20 miles east of where they started and 50 miles east of where they had thought they ought to be.

The news was so heartbreaking some men refused to believe it. It couldn't be. Worsley had made a mistake. But no. He obtained a third sight early in the afternoon which showed that Joinville Island, which had dropped from sight two weeks before, now was only 80 miles away.

Some unknown and undetectable easterly current had caught them—a current of such tremendous strength that it had driven them backward into the teeth of a gale.

To reach King George Island would mean sailing directly into that current, so for the third time Shackleton announced that the destination had been changed. This time it became Hope Bay, about 130 miles away at the tip of the Palmer Peninsula, beyond Joinville Island. The boats were set on a southerly course, and the men sat in almost absolute silence, tired through and discouraged, their hopes for an early landing completely shattered.

Late in the afternoon, the wind increased from the NNW, and the boats came upon some scattered ice which Shackleton thought might prove troublesome in the dark. He gave the order to heave to. They could not even find a floe large enough to accommodate Green and his stove—only a small chunk to which the *Docker* was made fast, with the *Wills* behind her and the *Caird* last.

Canvas from the tents was stretched over each boat and with great difficulty the small primus stoves were lighted so that some milk could be heated. They drank it scalding hot, huddled together under the flapping canvas of the tent cloths. They were thus enjoying the luxury of a moment's warmth, when a new menace appeared. Large blocks of ice began to drift around the edges of the floe to the lee side where the boats were tethered.

The tent cloths were thrown aside, and the men, using every available oar and boathook, positioned themselves around each boat and poled off the approaching chunks of ice, or held them at bay so that the boats would not be dashed against them in the swell. The struggle might have gone on all night. But about nine o'clock, in the space of only a few minutes, the wind suddenly veered around to the southwest. Immediately the floe ceased to provide a shelter and became instead a windward shore toward which the boats were being blown. Shackleton shouted to get away, and the oarsmen hurriedly got into position. It had happened so fast, and the wind was so strong, that there wasn't time even to get in the *Docker's* bow line that had secured them to the floe; it had to be cut. Then they pulled frantically until at last they were clear of the floe.

Again a thick, wet snow had begun to fall. The temperature, too, began to drop, with the wind blowing up from the pole. Before long, the surface of the sea was freezing into rubbery patches that would later become "pancake ice."

Shackleton ordered the *Docker* into the lead. The *Caird* was made fast to her stern, and the *Wills* brought up the rear. Two oars were put out from the *Docker* to keep the line of boats head up into the wind, and to prevent them from bumping into one another. By ten o'clock they were in position.

For the second night running, there was no sleep, though a few men snuggled together in hopes of generating enough warmth to drop off for a moment. But it was achingly cold. Hussey's thermometers were packed away so that no actual temperature reading could be taken, but Shackleton estimated it to be 4 below zero. They could even hear the water freezing. The snow fell on the newly formed ice with a tiny crackling sound, and the ice itself made a creaking hiss as it rose to the swell.

The clothes the men wore, now that they were sitting almost motionless, froze stiff. Not only were their garments wet from the spray and the snow, they were also worn and saturated with the oil secreted from the men's own bodies during six months of constant wear. If a man shifted his position, even slightly, his skin came in contact with a new, unwarmed surface of his clothing.

111

Thus everyone tried to sit absolutely still, but it could not be done. The weariness, the lack of food, the exertion, and the worry had weakened them so that the harder they tried to sit still, the more they shivered—and their own shivering kept them awake. It was better to row. Shackleton in the *Caird* doubted that some men would survive the night.

A hundred times, it seemed, Worsley was asked what time it was. Each time, he reached under his shirt and took out the chronometer he carried slung around his neck to keep it warm. Holding it up close to his face, he read its hands in the feeble light of the moon, shining through the thin snow clouds. In time, it became a kind of gruesome game—seeing who could hold out the longest before asking again what time it was. When finally somebody succumbed to the temptation, every head rose to await Worsley's answer.

But the dawn did come—at last. And in its light the strain of the long dark hours showed on every face. Cheeks were drained and white, eyes were bloodshot from the salt spray and the fact that the men had slept only once in the past four days. Matted beards had caught the snow and frozen into a mass of white. Shackleton searched their faces for an answer to the question that troubled him most: How much more could they take? There was no single answer. Some men looked on the point of breaking, while others showed an unmistakable determination to hold out. All of them at least had survived the night.

The *Endurance* heeled to port under pressure.

Feeding the dogs during the polar night.

Left: Pressure. Heavy floes of sea ice rafted up, with the trapped *Endurance* in the background.

Below: The end is near.

Below: Loading the *Caird*.

Left: Attempting to dig a sheltering cave on Elephant Island.

Marooned. Frank Wild (front row, second from the left) and most of the men left behind on Elephant Island.

Below: Camped on a floe. A drawing by George Marston.

Left: Decking over the
James Caird for the
journey to South Georgia.

Below: The first hot drink
in days, minutes after
the landing on Elephant Island.

Launching the *James Caird,* April 24, 1916.

Shortly after sunrise, the wind swung around to the southeast and freshened considerably. Shackleton called to Worsley to bring the *Docker* alongside the *Caird*. After a hurried conference, they announced that, for the fourth time, the destination was changed. In view of the southeast wind, they would run for Elephant Island once more, now 100 miles to the northwest—and pray God the wind held fair till they arrived.

After redistributing the stores so that the *Wills* was less crowded, the boats hoisted sail and set off with the *Caird* in the lead.

Toward eleven o'clock the scattered pack began to thin out, and all the while the wind was increasing. By late morning it had risen almost to gale force and was driving the boats along at a remarkable clip.

Just before noon they burst from the line of pack into the open sea.

The change was breathtaking. The northwest swell, which had been cushioned by the pack, now advanced upon the boats in undisguised immensity. Their course lay directly into it, and within minutes they were struggling up a hill of water whose face was a quarter mile long. At its summit the wind shrieked, blowing the spray into thin, feathery lines. Then they started down, a slow but steep descent into the valley leading to the next swell. Over and over again the cycle was repeated. Before long the pack was lost from sight, and occasionally one or another of the boats disappeared behind one of these enormous rolling hills of water.

113

It was as if they had suddenly emerged into infinity. They had an ocean to themselves, a desolate, hostile vastness. Shackleton thought of the lines of Coleridge:

"Alone, alone, all, all alone,
Alone on a wide wide sea."

They made a pitiable sight—three little boats, packed with the odd remnants of what had once been a proud expedition, bearing twenty-eight suffering men in one final, almost ludicrous bid for survival. But this time there was to be no turning back, and they all knew it.

The men clung to the sides of the pitching boats as they drove forward. Though they were making excellent headway, their progress was hard won. Both the *Docker* and the *Wills* were shipping water continually. The crews sat facing aft, with the wind directly in their faces—a position only slightly preferable to facing forward, where they would have been stung by the spray breaking over the side.

By midafternoon, the wind had risen even more, so Shackleton ordered a second reef taken in the sails, and they proceeded this way until dusk. At sunset, Worsley drew the *Docker* alongside the *Caird* and urged that they continue, but Shackleton flatly refused. It was difficult enough, he said, to keep the boats together in daylight; at night it would be impossible. He even rejected Worsley's suggestion that they join up and row during the night.

Shackleton was convinced that their best chance of reaching safety was to remain together. Both the *Caird* and the *Wills* were largely dependent on Worsley's skill as a navigator, and Shackleton was acutely aware that the *Wills* needed constant looking after. Not only was she the least seaworthy of the three boats, but Hudson, who was commanding her, was one of those less equal to the strain, and he was obviously weakening, both physically and mentally. Shackleton was certain the *Wills* would be lost if she got separated from the others.

He decided that the three boats would spend the night hove to. He ordered the *Docker* to rig a sea anchor, and the *Caird* made fast to the *Docker's* stern with the *Wills* behind her. Working with stiffening fingers, Worsley, Greenstreet, and McLeod lashed three oars together and stretched a piece of canvas across them. The contrivance was then made fast to a long piece of line and pitched over the side. They hoped the sea anchor would act as a brake, holding the bows of the boats up into the wind as it was dragged through the water. When it was in position, the crews of all three boats settled down to wait for morning.

It was a night almost to defy description. As the darkness deepened, the wind increased and the temperature dropped ever lower. Again an actual reading was impossible, but it was probably at least as low as 8 below. It was so cold that the seas that broke over them froze almost as soon as they hit. Even before the darkness was complete, it became apparent that the sea anchor could not hold them up into the wind effectively. The boats continually dropped off into the trough of the waves where they were swept broadside by the seas. The boats, the men—everything was soaked, then frozen. Most of the men tried to shelter themselves under the tent cloths, but the wind repeatedly tore them loose.

On the *Caird* they managed to make enough room for four men to huddle together at one time in the pile of sleeping bags in the bow, and they took turns trying in vain to sleep. On the *Docker,* however, there was only room enough for the men to sit upright, huddled together with their feet squeezed between the cases of stores. The seas that came on board ran down into the bottom of the boat, and since most of the men were wearing felt boots, their feet were soaked all night in the icy water. They did what they could to keep the boats bailed dry, but the water sometimes rose ankle-deep. To keep their feet from freezing, they worked their toes constantly inside their boots. They could only hope that the pain in their feet would continue, because comfort, much as they yearned for it, would mean that they were freezing. After a time, it took extreme concentration for them to keep wiggling their toes—it would have been so terribly easy just to stop.

By far the worst off of the boats was the *Wills.* The water she was shipping was sometimes almost knee-deep. Little Wally How, the seaman, found it impossible to drive from his mind the fear that a killer whale would upset them into the water. Stevenson, the fireman, periodically buried his face in his hands and wept. Blackboro, who had insisted on wearing leather boots to save his felt pair for what he thought would be the future, lost all feeling in his feet after several hours. And Hudson, who had been at the tiller for almost seventy-two hours straight, developed a pain in his left buttock which became increasingly intense as the part began to swell. After a time he had to sit hunched sideways, and the rolling of the boat was agony to him. He was also suffering from severe frostbite in his hands.

The line between the *Wills* and the *Caird* alternately tightened and slacked, dropping into the water and rising into the bitter cold air each time. As the hours passed, it accumulated an ever-thickening coat of ice. The lives of the eight men aboard the *Wills* depended on that line. If it parted, and it seemed almost certain to, the *Wills* would fall off into the trough of the sea and be swamped long before her crew could beat the ice off the sail and hoist it.

All the boats were thick with ice, but the *Wills* was weighted down like a log. The seas poured on board her, flowing over the pile of sleeping bags in the bow and leaving them sheathed in ice. Ice formed in masses around her bow as she dipped into each sea, weighting her down that much more, so that every half hour or oftener, men had to be sent forward to beat the ice off her bow lest she go under.

Finally, for all the party, there was thirst. They had left the pack so abruptly and unexpectedly that they had failed to take on board any ice to be melted into water. There had been nothing to drink since the previous morning, and the men were beginning to crave water desperately. Their mouths were dry and their half-frostbitten lips began to swell and crack. Some men, when they tried to eat, found it impossible to swallow, and their hunger brought on seasickness.

16

Gale Wind

TOWARD 3 A.M., the wind began to fall, and by five o'clock it had dropped to a gentle breeze. Gradually the sea grew calmer.

The sky was clear, and finally the sun rose in unforgettable brilliance through a pink mist along the horizon, which soon melted into flaming gold.

It was more than just a sunrise. It seemed to flood into their souls, rekindling the life within them. They watched the growing light quenching the wild, dark misery of the night that now, at last, was over.

As the sun climbed a fraction higher, they saw off the starboard bow the peaks of Clarence Island, and a little later, Elephant Island, dead ahead—the Promised Land, no more than 30 miles away. In the joy of that moment, Shackleton called to Worsley to congratulate him on his navigation, and Worsley, stiff with cold, looked away in proud embarrassment.

They would land by nightfall—provided that not a moment was lost. Shackleton, impatient to be on the move, gave the order to get underway immediately. But it was not that simple. The light of dawn revealed that many faces were marked by the ugly white rings of frostbite, and almost everyone was afflicted with salt-water boils that gave off a gray, curdlike discharge when they broke. McIlroy called to Shackleton from the *Wills* that Blackboro's feet apparently were gone because he had been unable to restore circulation in them. And Shackleton himself looked haggard. His voice, which was usually strong and clear, had grown hoarse with exhaustion. Both the *Docker* and the *Wills* were severely iced up, inside and out. It took more than an hour to chip away enough to make them fit for sailing.

The oars were frozen to the sides of the boats and had to be broken free. The men then tried to knock off their coating of ice, but two of them remained so slippery that they slid through the oarlocks and fell overboard. Fortunately the *Caird* managed to retrieve one, but the other drifted away.

The boats were finally underway at seven o'clock. A ration of nut food and biscuits was issued, but the men's thirst was now so intense that few of them could eat it. Shackleton suggested that they try chewing seal meat raw in order to swallow the blood. Pieces of the frozen meat were quickly handed out, and after several minutes of chewing and sucking, the men obtained enough of the bloody juice so they could at least swallow. But they went at it so voraciously that Shackleton realized the supply would soon be exhausted, so he ordered that the seal meat be given out only when thirst seemed to be threatening the reason of any individual.

The sails were set and they put out the oars and rowed at the same time, aiming for the west edge of Elephant

Island to offset the gentle southwest wind that was blowing.

In the *Docker,* both Macklin and Greenstreet took off their boots and found their feet frostbitten. Greenstreet's much worse than Macklin's. Orde-Lees offered to massage Greenstreet's feet. He worked over them for a long time; then he opened up his shirt and placed Greenstreet's half-frozen feet against the warmth of his bare chest. After a while, Greenstreet began to feel pain as the blood flowed back into the constricted vessels.

Hour after hour they rowed, and the outline of Elephant Island slowly grew larger. They had had no sleep for almost eighty hours, and their bodies had been drained of almost the last vestige of vitality. But the conviction that they had to land by nightfall gave rise to a strength born of desperation. It was pull or perish, and ignoring their sickening thirst, they leaned on their oars with what seemed the last of their strength.

By 2 P.M., the snowy, 3,500-foot peaks of Elephant Island rose steeply out of the water dead ahead, probably no more than ten miles off. But an hour later, the island was still in the same position, hanging there, no closer and yet no farther away. Row as they might, they were standing still, apparently caught in a strong tidal current setting offshore.

By 5 P.M., they were no closer, though they pulled frantically in the gathering dusk, hoping to make a landing before night. Half an hour later the wind suddenly sprang up out of the wsw, and within fifteen minutes it was blowing nearly 50 miles an hour. Worsley brought the *Docker* alongside the *Caird*. Screaming to make himself heard above the wind, he told Shackleton he thought it would be best if the boats separated to try to make land independently along the southeast shore of Elephant Island.

Shackleton, for once, agreed to the separation; at least, he granted Worsley permission to proceed independently. The *Wills,* however, was kept fast astern of the *Caird,* and Shackleton admonished Worsley to do everything in his power to stay within sight. It was dark by the time the *Docker* cast off.

The island was close, but just how close was now impossible to tell—maybe 10 miles, probably even less. High in the sky was a ghostly, pale white image, the light of the moon shining through the clouds and reflecting back up from the glaciers on the island. It was all they had to steer by as the boats pounded forward into the cross sea. At times the wind was so strong they had to let go the lines holding the sails to avoid capsizing. The men in the *Caird* crouched low to escape the driving spray, but in the *Docker,* and especially the *Wills,* there was no escape.

Their immediate goal was the southeast corner of the island. Once around that, they would have the protection of the land; then they could look for a place to beach the boats. About nine-thirty, the reflection in the sky looked very close, and they knew they were almost on top of the land. But then, inexplicably, they began to lose ground. Looking over the sides of the boats they could see that they were traveling rapidly through the water, yet ever so gradually the land was slipping from their grasp. There was nothing to do but to push on.

About midnight, Shackleton glanced to starboard and saw that the *Docker* was gone. He jumped to his feet and peered intently across the stormy waters, but there was no sign of her. Anxiously, he ordered the candle in the compass binnacle lighted and then had the binnacle hoisted up the mast so that it shone on the *Caird's* sail. But no answering light appeared in the distance.

Shackleton called for a box of matches. He instructed Hussey to light one every few minutes and hold it so that it flared against the sail. One at a time, Hussey struck the matches as Shackleton peered into the darkness. Still there was no signal from the *Docker*.

But she tried to answer. She was hardly more than a half mile away, and her men had seen the *Caird's* signal in the dark. On Worsley's instructions they took their only candle under the tent cloth and lighted it. Then they tried to hold it so that its light would show through the canvas in reply to Shackleton's signal—but the reply was never seen.

A moment later, all thought of trying to signal the *Caird* was forgotten as the *Docker* suddenly lurched violently in the grip of a fierce tide rip. Worsley was barely able to keep control of the boat. The crew hurriedly took in the sail and even unstepped the mast, which threatened to snap off in the wildly pitching boat. They put out the oars and tried to steady her by rowing.

Worsley ordered Orde-Lees to take up an oar, but Orde-Lees begged to be let off, claiming that he was not a fit rower for such a perilous time, and that it was too wet for him. The two men screamed at one another in the darkness, and from every corner of the boat men cursed Orde-Lees. But it was no use, and finally Worsley disgustedly waved him forward. Orde-Lees immediately crawled into the bottom and refused to move, even though his weight unbalanced the boat.

After a time, Worsley decided to risk hoisting sail again. He swung the *Docker* into the teeth of the wind, holding her as close to it as she would go, so that they were taking the seas more or less head on. He put all the skill of twenty-eight years at sea into holding her in that delicate position, but she was very nearly uncontrollable. Furthermore, she was becoming sluggish under her increasing burden of water. Orde-Lees—lying in the bottom—sat upright. He seemed to realize that the boat was sinking under him, and he grabbed a pot and began to bail. Cheetham joined him, and together they worked furiously, hurling the water over the side. In time, the *Docker* rose again to the seas.

It was now about three o'clock, and Worsley himself began to fail. He had faced the wind so long that his eyes refused to function properly, and he found it impossible to judge distance. Try as he might, he could no longer stay awake.

Now, seated at the tiller, his head began to nod. Macklin saw him going and offered to take over. Worsley agreed, but when he tried to go forward he found he could not straighten out his body. He had sat for almost six days in the same position. McLeod and Marston came aft and pulled him out of the stern, dragging him over the seats and cases of stores. Then they laid him down in the bottom of the boat and rubbed his thighs and stomach until his muscles began to loosen. But by then he was asleep.

Greenstreet, too, had taken a moment's exhausted rest, but now he awoke and took over the tiller from Macklin. Neither of them had any idea where they might be. But they shared the same dread as everybody else—the fear of being swept into the open sea.

The *Docker's* compass had been smashed some time earlier, and all that remained to steer by was Worsley's little silver pocket compass. The two men spread the tent cover over their heads, and Macklin struck matches while Greenstreet read the compass every few minutes in the hope of holding the *Docker* on a southwest course so that she would not be blown out to sea.

As they seemed on the very brink of exhaustion, and as the wind screamed to new heights, the palest hint of light showed in the eastern sky and began to brighten, very slowly. Even their raging thirst, after forty-eight hours without water, was forgotten as they waited for the sun to reveal their fate.

Gradually, the surface of the sea became discernible. And there, dead ahead, were the enormous gray-brown cliffs of Elephant Island—and less than a mile away.

The feeling of inexpressible relief was short-lived because just then, without an instant's warning, offshore gusts of wind swept down off the cliffs, striking the surface of the sea at perhaps 100 miles an hour. A moment later a wall of water as high as the boat rolled toward the *Docker*.

Greenstreet shouted to drop the sail. The oars were hurriedly put out and they pulled head-on into the blasts that shrieked down off the mountaintops. Somehow they managed to hold the *Docker's* head up into it, but the exertion required them to put forth strength they no longer really had. Looking forward, they saw a new wave, possibly 6 feet high, bearing down upon them.

Somebody shouted to wake up Worsley, and McLeod shook him violently, trying to rouse him. But Worsley was like a dead man, sprawled over the cases of stores midships with the soaking wet tent cloth spread over him. McLeod shook him again, and when Worsley failed to stir, McLeod kicked him, again and again; finally Worsley opened his eyes. He sat up, and instantly he realized what was happening.

"For God's sake," he shouted, "get her around—get away from it! Hoist the sail!"

Greenstreet put the tiller over, and the men struggled feverishly to raise the sail. She had just caught the wind when the first wave hit them and rolled over the stern. Greenstreet was almost knocked off his seat. A moment later, the second wave engulfed them. The *Docker*, half-filled with water, slumped under the burden and lost most of her headway. Everything else was forgotten. The men seized the first thing that came to hand and began to bail. They threw the water over the side with mugs, hats, even their cupped bare hands. Gradually they got the *Docker* emptied out. Worsley took the tiller and turned north to run before the gale, with the seas pursuing the boat from astern. He guided her close inshore, just under the lofty glaciers fringing the island. Pieces of ice floated amongst the waves, and the men leaned over the sides as the boat drove past and scooped them up with their hands.

A moment later they were chewing and sucking greedily, and the delicious water was running down their throats.

17

Land!

ALL DURING THE LONG NIGHT, Shackleton on board the *Caird* had kept watch for the *Docker*. And as the hours passed, his anxiety mounted. He had faith in Worsley's seamanship, but such a night demanded something more than skill.

However, there was more than enough to keep him occupied with the *Caird*. Wild remained at the tiller, and as the southwest gale increased, he held them on a course as nearly into the wind as possible so that they wouldn't be blown past the island. Spray burst over the bow and swept across the dark forms of the men huddled in the bottom of the boat.

On board the *Wills*, towed astern of the *Caird*, conditions were even more miserable. The pain in Hudson's side had become almost intolerable, and it was more than he could bear to stay at the tiller. Tom Crean took over for him, and occasionally Billy Bakewell had a turn at steering. Rickenson, a slight individual, seemed on the point of collapse, and sat by himself off to one side. How and Stevenson, when they weren't bailing, clung to one another seeking to generate some bit of warmth between their bodies.

The bow of the *Wills* plunged into almost every sea, so that the men sat knee-deep in water. Ironically, this was almost a comfort, for the water was warmer than the air. Blackboro's feet were long since beyond the point of hurting. He never complained, though he knew that it was only a matter of time until gangrene set in. Even if he lived, it seemed unlikely that this youngster who had stowed away a year and a half before would ever walk again. Once during the night, Shackleton called to him in an attempt to raise his spirits.

"Blackboro," he shouted in the darkness.

"Here, sir," Blackboro replied.

"We shall be on Elephant Island tomorrow," Shackleton yelled. "No one has ever landed there before, and you will be the first ashore."

Blackboro did not answer.

Shackleton sat in the stern of the *Caird* alongside Wild, with his hand on the line between them and the *Wills*, and he could feel the *Wills* seize up on the towline as she rose unwillingly to each wave. Looking back he could just see her in the darkness. Several times the line went slack and she disappeared from sight only to reappear suddenly, outlined against the whiteness of a breaking wave.

When at last the first gray tinge of dawn appeared, the *Wills*, by some marvelous caprice of luck, was still doggedly astern of the *Caird*. And there was land, too, looming on top of them off the port bow—great black headlands appearing through the mists, scarcely a quarter mile away. Immediately, Shackleton ordered them to put about and head west across the wind. And in the space of fifteen minutes, possibly less, the wind suddenly eased off. They had passed the northeast tip of the island —and they were under the lee of the land at last. They held to a westerly course with the hulking cliffs and glaciers rearing up alongside them. But there was absolutely no sign of a landing place—not even the smallest cove or beach.

There was ice, though. Large pieces of glaciers that had tumbled into the water floated on the surface. The men snatched up small chunks and thrust them into their mouths. Yet for nearly an hour they sailed westward searching the shoreline for a foothold, however small. Finally somebody spied a tiny, shingled beach, half-hidden behind a chain of rocks. Shackleton stood up on one of the seats and saw that it was a treacherous place. He hesitated for a moment, then ordered the boats to make for it.

When they were a thousand yards off, Shackleton signaled the *Wills* to come alongside and take him on board. Of the two boats, she had the shallower draft, and Shackleton wanted to approach the beach in her first to see if the *Caird* could negotiate the seething channel between the rocks.

At that exact moment, the *Docker* was driving westward along the coast, looking for a place to land. Since sunrise, by Worsley's estimate, they had gone 14 miles, past point after point, without seeing a single site fit to beach the boat on. During all that distance, there had not been a glimpse of the other two boats, and it was now almost nine-thirty. The *Docker's* crew were sure that they alone had survived the night. "Poor blighters," Greenstreet whispered to Macklin. "They're gone."

Then they rounded a tiny spit of land, and there, dead ahead, were the masts of the *Caird* and *Wills,* bobbing in the backwash from the breakers. By some incredible coincidence, the *Docker's* inability to find a suitable place to land had reunited her with the rest of the party. Had there been a haven somewhere in those 14 miles behind her, the two groups might now have been miles apart, each assuming the other had been lost.

The men aboard the *Docker* gave three hoarse cheers to their shipmates, but the noise of the breakers drowned them out. A few minutes later their sail was sighted from the *Caird,* and just then Shackleton himself looked up and saw the *Docker* bearing down upon them. By then the *Wills* was close inshore. A shallow reef lay across the opening, and heavy rollers foamed over it. Shackleton waited for his moment, then gave the order to pull, and the *Wills* rolled safely over the reef. With the next wave, her bow ground against the shore.

Shackleton, remembering his promise, urged Blackboro to jump ashore, but the lad failed to move. He seemed not to comprehend what Shackleton was saying. Impatiently, Shackleton took hold of him and lifted him over the side. Blackboro dropped to his hands and knees, then rolled over and sat down with the surf surging around him.

"Get up," Shackleton ordered.

Blackboro looked up. "I can't, sir," he replied.

Shackleton suddenly remembered Blackboro's feet. In the excitement of the landing he had forgotten, and he felt ashamed. How and Bakewell jumped overboard and pulled Blackboro farther up the beach.

The stores were rapidly unloaded, and the *Wills* was rowed out to the *Docker*. Stores and men were transferred and ferried ashore. Then the *Caird* was unloaded enough so she could negotiate the reef.

As the boats were being pulled to safety, Rickenson suddenly turned pale, and a minute later collapsed of a heart attack. Greenstreet's frostbitten feet would hardly support him, and he hobbled ashore and lay down alongside of Blackboro. Hudson pulled himself through the surf, then sank down on the beach. Stevenson, a vacant expression on his face, was helped ashore, out of reach of the water.

They were on land.

It was the merest handhold, 100 feet wide and 50 feet deep. A meager grip on a savage coast, exposed to the full fury of the sub-Antarctic Ocean. But no matter—they were on land. For the first time in 497 days they were on land. Solid, unsinkable, immovable, blessed land.

18

To Sea Again

MANY OF THE MEN half-stumbled aimlessly about, scuffling their feet in the pebbles, or bending down to pick up a handful of rocks; some even dropped full length to the ground to feel its sublime solidity beneath them. For a time a few men simply sat down, shivering uncontrollably and mumbling gibberish to themselves.

Just then the sun came out. In its light their faces showed dead white from exhaustion and frostbite, and from being continually soaked with water. The circles around their eyes were so deep their eyes seemed to have sunk slightly into their heads.

Green readied some milk as quickly as he could, and each man's mug was filled. They drank it almost boiling hot and its heat spread throughout their bodies, setting their nerves to tingling as if their blood had suddenly been thawed and begun to flow again.

Shackleton stood in the center of the group. He had removed his helmet and his long, uncut hair hung down over his forehead. His shoulders were bent with care, and his voice was so hoarse from shouting that he was unable to speak above a whisper. Yet he felt a profound sense of satisfaction and accomplishment to be standing at last on land, surrounded by his men.

The men themselves spoke very little as they drank their milk. Each seemed absorbed in his own thoughts. Most of them were extremely unsteady, both from exhaustion and from the fact that they had fought the motion of the boats so long that their equilibrium was temporarily unbalanced. When they had finished their milk, a party was sent to bring in some seals lying down the beach, from which thick steaks were cut.

Finally the food was ready, and they ate. It was neither breakfast nor lunch nor dinner. It was one long intermittent meal. As soon as they had finished the first round of steaks, Green put more on the fire. When these were ready the men stopped whatever they were doing and ate again. It wasn't until nearly 3 P.M. that they had eaten all they could hold.

Then it was time to sleep. They unrolled their soaked sleeping bags and wrung out what water they could; the dampness that remained made little difference. James wrote: "Turned in and slept, as we had never slept before, absolute dead dreamless sleep, oblivious of wet sleeping bags, lulled by the croaking of the penguins." It was the same for all of them. "How delicious," wrote Hurley, "to wake in one's sleep and listen to the chanting of the penguins mingling with the music of the sea. To fall asleep and awaken again and feel this is real. We have reached the land!!"

Most of the men were awakened once during that glorious night to stand an hour's watch, and even this

133

was almost pleasure. The night was calm, and the sky was clear. The moon shone on the little pebbled beach, washed by the waves, a scene of utter tranquility. Furthermore, wrote Worsley, the watchmen, during their one-hour tour of duty, "feed themselves, keep the blubber fire going, feed themselves, dry their clothes, feed themselves, and then feed themselves again before turning in."

Shackleton permitted the men to sleep until nine-thirty the next morning. But at breakfast an ugly rumor began to circulate, and when they had finished eating, Shackleton confirmed the almost shocking truth of it. They would have to move.

There could hardly have been a more demoralizing prospect. Having barely escaped the sea's hungry grasp a scant twenty-four hours before, now to have to return to it. . . . But the need was indisputable. They could see that only great good fortune had permitted them to land where they were. The cliffs at the head of the beach bore the marks of high tides and the scars of storm damage, indicating that the entire spit was frequently swept by seas. The place was obviously tenable only in good weather and while the tides were moderate.

Shackleton ordered Wild to take a crew of five seamen in the *Wills* and sail west along the coast to look for a more secure campsite. The *Wills* set out at eleven o'clock. She did not return until after dark and Wild's party confirmed the fact that this was truly an inhospitable place. In nine hours of looking, they had found only one seemingly secure place to camp—a fairly sheltered spit of beach, about 150 yards long and 30 yards wide, some 7 miles along the coast to the west. There was a good-sized penguin rookery there, Wild said, and his men had also sighted a number of seals and some few sea elephants. A nearby glacier would keep them supplied with ice for melting into water.

Shackleton was satisfied, and he announced that they would break camp at dawn. The party was awakened at 5 A.M., but the tide rose very slowly and it wasn't until eleven o'clock that there was enough water over the reef to get away.

Altogether, the journey took more than four hours—and the best that could be said of it was that it was nightmarish. All three of the boats just barely escaped being blown out to sea when they were caught by a series of so-called williwaws—violent, 150-mile-an-hour downdrafts characteristic of coastal areas in polar regions—that shrieked down off the mountains. In addition, Greenstreet very nearly froze his hands because he lost his mittens, and Macklin too suffered severely from frostbite when one of his mittens slipped off. He dared not stop rowing even long enough to replace it.

But toward four o'clock, they finally reached their new location and hauled the boats clear of the water.

19

Decision

ONCE MORE they were all on land, and safe. But the wondrous joy that had marked the landing only thirty hours before was absent now. They realized, as one man said, that "Elephant Island had flattered only to deceive." She had revealed her true face to them, and the sight of it was ugly.

Moreover, an examination of the new campsite raised serious doubts about whether it had been worth the trouble to move.

"A more inhospitable place could scarcely be imagined," wrote Macklin. "The gusts increased in violence and became so strong that we could hardly walk against them, and there was not a lee or a scrap of shelter anywhere." The wind was so strong they could not even pitch the tents, so they simply spread out their sleeping bags, then lay down and fell asleep.

Throughout the night the wind continued to shriek down from the mountains, and the blizzard persisted throughout that day, and into the next. Hardly a man stirred from the meager protection of his sleeping bag until 11 A.M., when Shackleton ordered all hands out to kill penguins. Orde-Lees wrote: "The blizzard was, if anything, worse. It was impossible to face the wind.

The driving snow rushed down one's throat as one breathed and choked one." But somehow they managed to secure a total of seventy-seven penguins altogether. "Skinning them with our already partially frostbitten hands was painful work," Orde-Lees continued, "for to bare the hand for very few minutes in such a blizzard means almost certain frostbite. We sought shelter as we could find . . . but it was only the warmth of the dead penguins that saved our hands."

The weather cleared briefly during the night, and the hulking cliffs of the island stood out in silhouette against the star-filled sky. By morning, a fresh blizzard had begun, but it was not quite so bad as the last one.

It was April 20, a day notable for only one reason: Shackleton finally made official what everyone had expected for a long time. He would take a party of five men and set sail in the *Caird* for South Georgia to bring relief. They would leave as soon as the *Caird* could be made ready and provisioned for the trip.

The news came as no surprise to anyone. In fact even a formal announcement was unnecessary. The subject had been discussed openly even long before the party had left Patience Camp. They knew that whatever island they might ultimately reach, a boat journey of some sort would be necessary to bring rescue to the party as a whole. Even the destination, illogical as it might look on a map, had been settled to everyone's satisfaction.

There were three possible objectives. The nearest of these was Cape Horn, the island of Tierra del Fuego—

"Land of Fire," which lay about 500 miles to the north-west. Next was the settlement of Port Stanley in the Falkland Islands, some 550 miles very nearly due north. Finally there was South Georgia, slightly more than 800 miles to the northeast. Though the distance to South Georgia was more than half again as far as the journey to Cape Horn, weather conditions made South Georgia the most sensible choice.

An easterly current, said to travel 60 miles a day, prevails in the Drake Passage, and almost incessant gales blow in the same direction. To reach either Cape Horn or the Falkland Islands would mean beating to windward against both of these colossal forces; it was enough to dare a 22-foot boat on these storm-wracked waters without trying to drive her to windward. En route to South Georgia, on the other hand, the prevailing winds would be generally astern—at least in theory.

All this had been discussed and discussed again. And though the *Caird's* chances of actually reaching South Georgia were remote, a great many men genuinely wanted to be taken along. The prospect of staying behind, of waiting and not knowing, of possibly wintering on this hateful island was far from attractive.

Shackleton had already made up his mind, after long discussions with Wild, not only as to who should be taken, but who should not be left behind. Worsley would be indispensable. They would travel perhaps a thousand miles across the stormiest ocean on the globe. The ultimate goal was an island no more than 25 miles wide at its widest point. To guide an open boat that distance,

138

under conditions that were frightening even to contemplate, and then to strike a pinpoint on the chart was a task that would sorely tax even Worsley's skill as a navigator. After him, Shackleton chose Crean, McNeish, Vincent, and McCarthy.

Crean was tough, a seasoned sailor; but more important, Shackleton was not sure that Crean's rough, tactless nature would lend itself well to a period of enforced and perhaps protracted waiting. McNeish was now fifty-seven years old, and really not up to the journey. But both Shackleton and Wild felt that the dour old carpenter was a potential troublemaker and not a good man to be left behind. Jack Vincent bore the same stigma as McNeish—his compatibility under trying conditions was open to doubt. By contrast, Shackleton picked well-liked Timothy McCarthy for no more complicated reasons than that he was an experienced seaman and that he was built like a bull.

As soon as Shackleton made the decision official, McNeish and Marston went to work removing the planks that had been added to the *Docker* in order to fashion a sort of decking over the *Caird*. The blizzard made working conditions miserable. They also attached the runners of a dismantled sledge across the upper sides of the boat to form a framework for decking her over. Pieces of plywood from the cases of stores were nailed over these, and a canvas covering of sorts was begun. The mainmast was removed from the *Docker* and lashed inside the *Caird's* keel in the hope that she would not break in two when she encountered bad weather.

Greenstreet's frostbitten hands had recovered some-what, and he and Bakewell were given the job of pro-viding the *Caird* with ballast. Together they sewed shale into canvas sacks, about a hundred pounds to each sack. The canvas was frozen, and they had to thaw it out a foot at a time by holding it close to the blubber stove. The heat and the rough stones caused the frostbite blisters in Greenstreet's hands to break and then bleed.

The next day the blizzard rose to new heights. Several men were cut on the face by bits of flying ice and rock. All work except the simplest cooking was out of the ques-tion, and the men stayed in their sleeping bags all day. Wild predicted that if conditions didn't improve shortly, some of the weaker men would not survive. Fortunately the wind eased considerably during the night, and in the morning McNeish got busy once more with the *Caird*.

Shackleton spent the days supervising the various ac-tivities. He saw that the *Caird* was very nearly finished, and announced that she would sail as soon as the weather permitted. As evening came on and the weather looked more promising, Shackleton ordered Orde-Lees and Vin-cent to melt ice to fill the two water casks to be carried aboard the *Caird*. They made every effort to find fresh-water ice from the glacier, but all of it had been tainted slightly by frozen salt-water spray.

Shackleton spent almost the whole night talking with Wild about a hundred different subjects, ranging from what should be done in the event that a rescue party failed to arrive within a reasonable length of time to the dis-tribution of tobacco. When there was nothing more to discuss, Shackleton wrote a letter in his log, which he left with Wild:

April 23rd, 1916 Elephant Island
Dear Sir

In the event of my not surviving the boat journey to South Georgia you will do your best for the rescue of the party. You are in full command from the time the boat leaves this island, and all hands are under your orders. On your return to England you are to communicate with the Committee. I wish you, Lees & Hurley to write the book. You watch my interests. In another letter you will find the terms as agreed for lecturing you to do England Great Britain & Continent. Hurley the U.S.A. I have every confidence in you and always have had, May God prosper your work and your life. You can convey my love to my people and say I tried my best.

Yours sincerely

E. H. SHACKLETON

FRANK WILD

20

The Departure

THROUGHOUT THE NIGHT the successive watchmen kept a close watch for a break in the weather; it came during the very early morning hours. The wind moderated considerably. Shackleton was immediately notified and he ordered that all hands be called at the first streak of light. The men were turned out just before 6 A.M., and they began to collect stores and equipment for the boat.

The *Caird* party was to take a six weeks' supply of food, consisting of three cases of the scrupulously hoarded sledging ration, two cases of nut food, a supply of biscuits, and powdered milk and bouillon cubes to provide the party with hot drinks. The cooking would be done on a Primus stove, and two were to be taken so there would be a spare. What little extra clothing could be found in the way of socks and mittens was rounded up, along with six of the reindeer sleeping bags.

For equipment, the *Caird* would carry one pair of binoculars, a prismatic compass, a small medicine chest, four oars, a bailer, the pump that Hurley had made, a shotgun and some shells, a sea anchor and a fishing line, plus a few candles and a supply of matches. Worsley had gathered together all the navigational aids he could find. He took his own sextant and another which belonged to Hudson, along with the necessary navigational tables and what charts were to be had. These were packed into a box that was made as watertight as possible. He still carried his sole chronometer slung around his neck. Out of twenty-four on board the *Endurance* when she sailed from England, this one alone had survived.

A farewell breakfast was prepared, for which Shackleton permitted two extra biscuits and a quarter pound of jam per man. For the most part, the men stood around joking. McCarthy was admonished by the other forecastle hands not to get his feet wet during the voyage. Worsley was cautioned against overeating when he reached civilization, and Crean was forced to promise that he would leave some girls for the rest of the party after they were rescued. But the tension in the air was unmistakable. Both groups knew they might very well never see one another again.

Toward nine o'clock McNeish reported to Shackleton that the boat was ready. Under the circumstances McNeish had done a magnificent job. The entire boat was decked over with canvas except for an open hatchway aft that was about 4 feet long and 2 feet wide. Yoke lines like reins ran back to the rudder for steering. So far as appearances went, she looked seaworthy enough.

The *Caird's* crew climbed on board, and she was then paddled out past the reef. She waited there at the end of her bowline while the *Wills* was launched and loaded with about half a ton of ballast. This cargo was rowed out and transferred to the *Caird;* on her second trip, the *Wills* took out another quarter ton of ballast sacks, and an extra 500 pounds of large rocks.

Shackleton was now ready to go. He had spoken to Wild for the last time and the two had shaken hands. The provisions were placed on board the *Wills.* Then Shackleton climbed aboard and she pulled away from the beach.

"Good luck, Boss," the shore party called after him. Shackleton swung around and waved briefly.

When they reached the *Caird,* Shackleton and Vincent jumped on board, and the stores were rapidly passed across.

The *Wills* then returned and the two 18-gallon casks of water were made fast to her stern. One of them tore loose crossing the reef, but the *Wills* recovered it and returned with it to the *Caird.*

For a few minutes, the two boats lay alongside one another, bumping heavily. Finally the two crews leaned across and shook hands. Then the *Wills* let go and headed for the beach.

It was just twelve-thirty. The three little sails on the *Caird* were up when the men ashore saw McCarthy in the bow signaling to cast off the bow line. Wild let go of it, and McCarthy hauled it in. The party on shore gave three cheers, and across the surging breakers they heard three small shouts in reply.

The *Caird* caught the wind, and Worsley at the helm swung her bow toward the north.

"They made surprising speed for such a small craft," Orde-Lees recorded. "We watched them until they were out of sight, which was not long, for such a tiny boat was soon lost to sight on the great heaving ocean; as she dipped into the trough of each wave, she disappeared completely, sail and all."

21

A Tireless Enemy

THE LITTLE GROUP of dark figures waving good-by were silhouetted against the white snow, and they made a pathetic picture from the *Caird* as she lifted to the increasing swell.

Worsley held her on a northerly course and it was just two o'clock when she reached the ice surrounding Elephant Island. It proved to be a thick line of ancient floes and Worsley swung the boat east, parallel with the ice, to search for an opening. They found one, though it was nearly clogged with floe fragments and patches of brash ice. The sails were dropped and the men carefully crawled up onto the decking and put out their oars. After rowing for an hour they came to the northern edge of the pack, then emerged into the open sea.

The wind had gradually swung around to the southeast, the perfect direction for driving them north. Shackleton ordered the sails set, and then sent Crean, McNeish, Vincent, and McCarthy forward to get some sleep, saying that he and Worsley would stay on duty throughout the night to watch for ice.

When everything was squared away, Shackleton turned and looked astern. It was just possible to make out

Elephant Island as a hulking, shadowy mass. For several minutes he stared without speaking.

A forbidding-looking place, certainly, but that only made it seem the more pitiful. It was the refuge of twenty-two men who, at that very moment, were camped on a precarious, storm-washed spit of beach, as helpless and isolated from the outside world as if they were on another planet. Their plight was known only to the six men in this ridiculously little boat, whose responsibility now was to prove that all the laws of chance were wrong —and return with help. It was a staggering trust.

As the darkness deepened the two men sat side by side, Worsley steering and Shackleton huddled close up against him. Their primary concern was ice, and though they passed an occasional lump early in the evening, by ten o'clock the sea appeared to be clear.

From time to time Shackleton rolled cigarettes for both of them, and they spoke of many things. It was obvious that the burden of responsibility Shackleton had borne for sixteen months had nibbled away somewhat at his enormous self-confidence. He wanted to talk and to be assured that he had acted wisely.

He confided to Worsley that the decision to separate the party had been a desperately difficult one, and he abhorred having to make it. But somebody had to go for help, and this was not the sort of responsibility which could be delegated to another person.

As for the journey itself, he seemed strangely doubtful, and he asked Worsley's opinion of their chances. Worsley replied that he was sure that they would make it, but it was evident that Shackleton was far from convinced.

The truth was that he felt rather out of his element. He had proved himself on land. He had demonstrated there beyond all doubt his ability to pit his matchless tenacity against the elements—and win. But the sea is a different sort of enemy. Unlike the land, where courage and the simple will to endure can often see a man through, the struggle against the sea is an act of physical combat, and there is no escape. It is a battle against a tireless enemy in which man never actually wins; the most that he can hope for is not to be defeated.

It gave Shackleton a feeling of uneasiness. He now faced an adversary so formidable that his own strength was nothing in comparison, and he did not enjoy being in a position where boldness and determination count for almost nothing, and in which victory is measured only in survival. But more than anything he was dreadfully tired, and he wanted simply for the journey to be over, and as quickly as possible.

Just before six o'clock, the first light of dawn crept across the sky, and as it grew brighter both men relaxed. Now if they came upon any ice, at least they could see it.

After breakfast Shackleton announced that the watches would begin, four hours on and four hours off. Shackleton said he would take the first trick with Crean and McNeish, and Worsley would have the other with Vincent and McCarthy.

22

Ordeal

To CLASSIFY THE DANGERS they faced in order of magnitude would be impossible, but of the known threats, the greatest undoubtedly was ice—especially at night. One single collision with an unseen fragment could end the journey in a moment. Thus Shackleton's plan was to get north with all possible speed before turning east toward South Georgia.

And for the next two days they were lucky. The wind held steady out of the southwest—much of the time almost at gale force. By noon on April 26, they had logged a total of 128 miles from Elephant Island without encountering a sign of ice.

Those two days, however, were an ordeal during which they were introduced, one at a time, to the endless miseries which constituted life on board the boat. Always and forever there was the water—the all-pervading, inescapable water. Sometimes it was just a shower of spray thrown up from the bow and flung astern by the wind, which caused no real suffering except to the man at the helm. Much worse were the quieter, solid seas dipped up by the bow that poured aft and sloshed into the cockpit. And worst of all were the occasions when the

149

boat plunged down just as a wave broke. Then green, foaming water rolled across the decking, splashed into the cockpit and drained down into the boat in icy streams through a score of openings in the canvas decking, as rain might pour through the roof of some dilapidated shack. Within twenty-four hours after leaving Elephant Island, the decking had begun to sag so that there were a dozen pockets to hold the water.

The man at the helm, of course, suffered the most, and each of them took his turn at the yoke lines for an hour and twenty minutes during each watch. But the other two men on duty were better off only by comparison. When they weren't bailing or tending the sails or shifting ballast by moving the rocks in the bottom, they spent their time trying to avoid the streams coming from above. It was of little use, though. Invariably they wound up huddled over with the water pouring off their backs.

All of them were dressed more or less the same way— heavy wool underwear, woolen trousers, a thick, loose sweater, with a pair of light gabardine Burberry over-alls on the outside. Their heads were covered with knitted, woolen helmets and Burberry outer helmets, tucked in at the neck. On their feet they wore two pairs of socks, a pair of ankle-high felt boots and finneskoes— reindeer-skin boots with the hair side out, though every trace of hair had long since worn off, leaving them bald and limp. There was not a set of oilskins on board.

Such clothing was intended for wear in intense, dry cold—not on board a pitching, spray-drenched boat. Here it had an almost wicklike action, soaking up every icy drop until the saturation point was reached, then maintained.

The best that could be done was to live with this trial by water, as they had on the trip to Elephant Island—to sit as still as possible after each soaking so as to avoid contact with the newly drenched area of clothing. But to sit motionless in a 22-foot boat in a heavy sea can be difficult indeed.

The boat had to be pumped out at fairly frequent intervals, usually two or three times each watch, and the job required two men—one to operate the plunger while the other held the icy brass cylinder down into the water in the bottom of the boat. Even with mittens, the hands of the man gripping the cylinder would go numb within the space of five minutes, and they would trade places.

Nor was the discomfort on board limited to the men on watch. They realized from the very beginning that even sleeping had a special brand of unpleasantness all its own. The sleeping bags were located in the bow, nominally the driest part of the boat. To reach them involved a tortuous crawl on hands and knees over the rocks in the bottom. The closer a man got to the bow, the more restricted the space became, until finally he had to get down on his belly and slither forward, insinuating himself between the underside of the seats and the ballast.

When at last he had reached the bow, there was the job of getting into his bag, then finally the problem of going to sleep. Fatigue helped, of course, but even so, the action of the boat in the bow was more violent than anywhere else. At times they were heaved bodily upwards, only to fall down onto the rocks again, or perhaps to be slammed from beneath as the boat was pitched aloft by a new wave. The *Caird* had been equipped with six sleeping bags so that each man might have his own. But Shackleton soon suggested that they share three bags and use the others as mattresses, to protect them from the rocks. Everyone quickly agreed.

They discovered, too, that under the decking there was not quite enough room to sit upright. For the first couple of meals they tried to eat half bent over, with their chins pressed down against their chests. But this position greatly interfered with swallowing, and the only thing to do was to stretch out on the rocks in the bottom

But no matter what position they assumed—sitting, reclining, or lying in their sleeping bags—the struggle against the motion of the boat was ceaseless. The 2,000 pounds of ballast in the bottom gave the *Caird* a particularly vicious action, and she jerked upright after every wave. Worsley thought she was over-ballasted and he urged Shackleton to throw some of the rocks overboard. But Shackleton took a characteristically cautious view of the matter. The only way to see if Worsley was right was to dump the ballast—and then it would be gone forever. It was better, Shackleton felt, to put up with the wicked motion of the boat than to risk being light.

They had sailed from Elephant Island in rather high spirits, knowing that they were embarked at last for civilization. As McNeish had recorded—"wet through, but happy through it all."

But after two days of uninterrupted misery, their

cheeriness had worn away. And by noon on April 26, after Worsley had fixed the position at 128 miles from Elephant Island, the ordeal to which they were committed had become altogether too real. There was only the consolation that they were making progress—at the agonizingly slow rate of about 1 mile every half hour or so.

The actual position on April 26 was 59°46′ South, 52°18′ West, and it put the *Caird* a scant 14 miles north of the 60th parallel of latitude. Thus they had just crept over the line separating the "Raving Fifties" from the "Screaming Sixties," so called because of the weather that prevails there.

This, then, was the Drake Passage, the most dreaded bit of ocean on the globe—and rightly so. Here nature has been given a proving ground on which to demonstrate what she can do if left alone. The results are impressive.

It begins with the wind. There is an immense area of persistent low pressure in the vicinity of the Antarctic Circle, approximately 67° South latitude. It acts as a giant sump into which high pressure from farther north continually drains, accompanied by almost ceaseless, gale-force, westerly winds. In the prosaic, often studiously understated language of the U.S. Navy's *Sailing Direction for Antarctica,* these winds are described categorically:

"They are often of hurricane intensity and with gust velocities sometimes attaining to 150 to 200 miles per hour. Winds of such violence are not known elsewhere, save perhaps within a tropical cyclone."

Also in these latitudes, as nowhere else on earth, the

153

sea girdles the globe, uninterrupted by any mass of land. Here, since the beginning of time, the winds have mercilessly driven the seas clockwise around the earth to return again to their birthplace, where they reinforce themselves or one another.

The waves thus produced have become legendary among seafaring men. They are called Cape Horn Rollers or "graybeards." Their length has been estimated from crest to crest to exceed a mile, and the terrified reports of some mariners have placed their height at 200 feet, though scientists doubt that they very often exceed 80 or 90 feet. How fast they travel is largely a matter of speculation, but many sailormen have claimed their speed occasionally reaches 55 miles an hour. Thirty knots is probably a more accurate figure.

Charles Darwin, on first seeing these waves breaking on Tierra del Fuego in 1833, wrote in his diary: "The sight . . . is enough to make a landsman dream for a week about death, peril and shipwreck."

As viewed from the *Caird*, the sight of these rollers constituted ample reason for such thoughts. In the rare moments when the sun shone, they were cobalt blue, which gave them the appearance of being infinitely deep —as indeed they were. But most of the time the sky was overcast, and then the whole surface of the sea turned a somber, lifeless gray.

There was no sound to the relentless advance of these cliffs of water except the hiss of their foaming brows when they rose to such a height or charged forward so fast that they lost their balance and their crests tumbled to the force of gravity.

Once every ninety seconds or less the *Caird's* sail would go slack as one of these gigantic waves loomed astern, possibly 50 feet above her, and threatening, surely, to bury her under a hundred million tons of water. But then, by some phenomenon of buoyancy, she was lifted higher and higher up the face of the onrushing swell until she found herself, rather unexpectedly, caught in the turmoil of foam at the summit and hurtling forward.

Over and over again, a thousand times each day, this drama was re-enacted. Before long, to the men on board the *Caird,* it lost all elements of awesomeness and they found it routine and commonplace instead, as a group of people may become inured to the perils of living in the shadow of an active volcano.

Only very occasionally did they think about South Georgia. It was so remote, so Utopian that it was almost depressing to contemplate. No man could have endured with just that to keep him going.

Instead, life was reckoned in periods of a few hours, or possibly only a few minutes—an endless succession of trials leading to deliverance from the particular hell of the moment. When a man was awakened to go on watch, the focal point of his existence became that time, four hours away, when he could slither back into the cold, wet rockiness of the sleeping bag he was now leaving. And within each watch there were a number of subdivisions: the time at the helm—eighty eonic minutes, during which a man was forced to expose himself to the full wickedness of the spray and the cold; the ordeal of pumping, and the awful task of shifting ballast; and the lesser trials which lasted perhaps two minutes—like the interval after each numbing spray struck until a man's clothes warmed enough so that he could move once more.

Again and again the cycle was repeated until the body and the mind arrived at a state of numbness in which the frenzied antics of the boat, the perpetual cold and wet came to be accepted almost as normal.

On April 27, three days out from Elephant Island, their luck turned bad, when the wind slowly moved around toward the north—dead ahead.

Because of the threat of ice, they could not afford to be blown a single mile to the south. Thus there was no choice but to hold the *Caird* up into the wind as best they could.

And so the struggle began, swinging from one tack to the other and absorbing punishment while doing nothing more than holding their own. But shortly after 11 P.M. the wind eased down and they were able to resume the course to the northeast.

Already, however, dangerous signs of deterioration were appearing. About mid-morning, McNeish sat down and peeled off his boots. His legs and feet were puffy and dead white, apparently from lack of exercise and from being continually soaked. The other men did likewise and they were all the same.

However, the damage to Worsley's navigational books by the constant soaking was an even more serious problem. The destruction of these books could mean losing the way across this forsaken waste of ocean. And though every effort was made to protect them, they had to be taken out whenever a sight was taken. And as a result they were fast approaching a state of pulpiness. Pages had to be carefully peeled apart to separate them.

In the matter of taking sights, Worsley at first tried bracing himself inside the cockpit. But it was no good. To remain upright was difficult enough; to get an accurate reading was impossible. He found that it was best to kneel on the helmsman's seat, with Vincent and McCarthy holding him around the waist.

Early in the afternoon of April 28, the wind slowly moved to the west and began to freshen.

The dawn of the fifth day, April 29, rose on a lumpy sea under a dull sky. Low, troubled clouds skudded past, almost touching the surface of the water. The wind was nearly dead astern, and the *Caird* labored forward like a protesting old woman being hurried along faster than she cared to go.

Just before noon a rift appeared in the sky, and Worsley hurriedly got his sextant. He was just in time, for a few minutes later the sun smiled down for one wintry flicker and then was gone. But Worsley had his sight, and when the position was worked out, it put the *Caird* at 58° 38' South, 50°0' West—they had covered 238 miles since leaving Elephant Island, six days before.

They were almost one-third of the way.

23

Heaved To

ONE-THIRD OF THE SENTENCE had been served.

Throughout the day and into the night, the south-westerly wind continued, growing ever stronger. By the time the bleak gray sky grew light on the morning of April 30, the surface of the sea was torn into foam, and the frenzied screech of the gale through the rigging rose and fell hysterically as the *Caird* was lifted to each successive swell. The temperature had dropped very close to zero, and the bitterness of the wind suggested that it was blowing straight off pack ice that was not very far away.

As the morning hours passed, it became more and more of a struggle to steer the boat. The 60-knot gale drove her head down into the seas, and the huge waves that rolled up astern constantly threatened to slew her around broadside. By midmorning she was wallowing more than sailing, running off to one side and then the other, and taking seas on board with almost every wave. The pump was not adequate to handle the water, and extra hands had to be called to bail. Toward noon the boat began to ice up.

The decision was inevitable, but Shackleton put it off as long as he dared. They pumped and bailed and beat the ice off her—but it was no use. The sea was more than she could take. The sails were dropped, and the sea anchor, a cone-shaped piece of canvas about 4 feet long, was put over on the end of a long bow line. It dragged through the water and thus brought the *Caird's* bow up into the wind.

Almost at once conditions improved. At least less water came on board. The boat, however, behaved like a thing possessed. She staggered drunkenly upward over each new wave, then plunged sideways only to have her bow jerked violently around as she seized up on the sea anchor. There was never a moment—not even an instant of repose. The only thing to do was to hang on, and endure.

It was not long before the furled sails started to collect ice, and with each burst of spray their load grew heavier. Within an hour, they were frozen into a solid mass, and the action of the boat was growing sluggish as she began to get top-heavy. The sails had to be removed, so Crean and McCarthy were sent forward, and after knocking off the ice, they brought the sails below and stuffed them into the already crammed space under the decking.

And so the night began. Each of the watches shivered through their four hideous hours, cringing beneath the decking, sodden and half-frozen, trying to remain upright against the wild lurching of the boat while perched on the despised rocks in the bottom.

For seven painful days the rocks had made eating difficult; they had interfered with bailing; they had vastly complicated the simple act of getting about, and they had made sleeping all but impossible. But it was moving them that was worst of all. Periodically they had to be shifted in order to ballast the boat properly, which meant lifting them while crouched over and kneeling, often painfully, on other rocks. By now, every sharp corner and every slippery surface was intimately known and utterly detested.

Then, too, there were the reindeer hairs. They moulted from the insides of the sleeping bags, and at first they had been only a petty annoyance. But no matter how much hair was shed, the supply seemed inexhaustible. And they were everywhere . . . the sides of the boat, the seats, the ballast. They clung in wet clumps to faces and hands. The men breathed them as they slept, and occasionally woke up choking on them. The hairs ran down into the bottom and clogged the pump, and little clusters of them were turning up more and more frequently in the food.

Gradually, as the long hours of the night crept by, a subtle change could be detected in the boat. For one thing, the trickles of water through the decking became smaller, then finally ceased altogether. At the same time her behavior was growing noticeably less violent, and instead of pitching wildly, she rose to the seas with increasing restraint.

The first light of dawn told why. The entire boat above the waterline was encased in ice, half a foot thick in places, and the rope to the sea anchor had grown to the size of a man's thigh. Under the weight of it, she was riding at least 4 inches deeper, like a waterlogged derelict rather than a boat.

Worsley was on watch and he immediately sent Mc-
Carthy to awaken Shackleton, who hurried aft. When he
saw the situation, he excitedly ordered all hands called.
Then he himself took a small axe and cautiously crawled
forward.

With extreme care so as not to puncture the decking,
he began to knock the ice away with the back side of the
axe. Periodically a wave burst against the boat and
swept over him, but he kept at it for nearly ten minutes
while the others anxiously looked on. By then he was
so stiff with cold that he could no longer trust his grip or
balance. He crawled back into the cockpit with the
water dripping from his clothes and his beard frozen half-
stiff. He was shivering noticeably as he handed the axe
to Worsley to continue the job, cautioning him to use
extreme care while he was on the decking.

And so each of them took his turn at chipping for as
long as he could endure it, which was rarely more than
five minutes. Below, Shackleton discovered that ice was
forming even inside the cockpit. Long icicles hung from
under the decking, and the water in the bottom was very
nearly frozen.

He called for Crean, and together they managed to get
the Primus stove alight in the hope that it would give off
enough heat to warm the cockpit above the freezing
point. Unless the water in the bottom could be thawed
enough so it could be pumped out, there was danger that
it would simply sink the boat under them.

It took an hour of agonizing work on deck before they
felt the *Caird* begin to regain her buoyancy. But they
kept at it until they had succeeded in getting rid of most

of the ice except a large chunk on the sea-anchor line which they simply could not risk attempting to reach.

Shackleton then called them below to have some milk. They gathered around the stove, almost sick with cold. It seemed inconceivable that their numbed bodies could have given off any warmth, but apparently they did, for after a while the icicles under the decking began to melt and drip down onto them. Not long afterward the water in the bottom had thawed enough so they could pump it out.

Throughout the afternoon they watched in helpless apprehension as the coating of ice steadily built up again. And late in the day Shackleton decided there was too much at stake to gamble on the chance that the *Caird* would survive until morning. Once more, he ordered that the boat be cleared. It took more than an hour, but finally it was done, and after a ration of hot milk they settled down to wait for morning.

The southwesterly gale screamed on, showing not the slightest sign of fatigue. The watches of that night were like a tally sheet of infinity. Every individual minute had to be noted, then lived through and finally checked off. There was not even a crisis to relieve the tortured monotony. When at last, about six o'clock, the sky to the east began to brighten they could see that once again the boat was carrying a dangerously heavy burden of ice. As soon as the light permitted she had to be chipped clear for the third time.

It was May 2, and the beginning of the third day of the gale. The weather throughout had been overcast so that no position could be obtained. Now the anxiety of not really knowing where they were was added to everything else.

Some time after nine o'clock, the wind eased ever so slightly, though nowhere near enough to get underway. A few minutes later the *Caird* rose to a particularly high sea, and just then she was struck by a breaking wave. The smallest quiver—a gentle shock—passed through her, and the wave rolled on. But this time she didn't swing back up into the wind. The sea anchor was gone.

24

The Great Wave

THERE WAS A MOMENT OF CON-
fusion; then they felt her roll sicken-
ingly to starboard as she fell off into the trough of the sea
and they knew instinctively what had happened.

Both Shackleton and Worsley scrambled to their feet
and saw the frayed end of the bow line dragging through
the water. The lump of ice was gone—and the sea
anchor with it.

Shackleton thrust his head below and shouted for the
others to get the jib. They hauled it out, frozen into
a rumpled mass. Crean and McCarthy crept forward
over the heavily rolling deck, dragging the sail with them.
The rigging, too, was frozen and had to be beaten into
compliance. But after a long minute or two they got
enough ice off the halyards to hoist the jib to the mainmast as a storm trysail.

Slowly, grudgingly, the *Caird's* bow once more swung
around into the wind, and all of them felt the tension go
out of their muscles.

The job of the helmsman now was to hold her as
close to the wind as she would go, swinging from one tack
to the other. It required constant vigilance, and it could

hardly have been more unpleasant, facing into the breaking seas and the piercing wind.

Fortunately the gale continued to diminish, and by eleven o'clock Shackleton decided to risk hoisting sail. Then, for the first time in forty-four hours, the *Caird* was underway again toward the northeast, and the journey was resumed. But it was a slovenly course, with the boat running before the enormous following sea, her bow half buried by the force of the wind astern.

Shortly after noon, as if from nowhere, a magnificent wandering albatross appeared overhead. In contrast to the *Caird,* the albatross soared with an ease and grace that was poetic, riding the gale on wings that never moved, sometimes dropping to within 10 feet of the boat, then rising almost vertically on the wind, a hundred, two hundred feet, only to plunge downward again in a beautifully effortless sweep.

It was perhaps one of nature's ironies. Here was her largest and most incomparable creature capable of flight, whose wingspread exceeded 11 feet from tip to tip, and to whom the most violent storm was meaningless, sent to accompany the *Caird,* as if in mockery of her painful struggles.

Hour after hour the albatross circled overhead, and there was an elegance of motion to the bird's flight that was very nearly hypnotic. The men could hardly avoid a feeling of envy. Worsley remarked that the albatross could probably have covered the distance to South Georgia in fifteen hours or less.

As if to emphasize their wretchedness, Worsley recorded: "Reindeer bags in such a hopeless sloppy slimy mess, smelling badly & weighing so heavily that we throw two of the worst overboard." Each of them weighed about 40 pounds.

Later he wrote: "Macty [McCarthy] is the most irrepressable optimist I've ever met. When I relieve him at the helm, boat iced & seas pourg: down yr neck he informs me with a happy grin 'It's a grand day sir' I was feeling a bit sour just before. . . ."

Throughout the afternoon and evening the weather gradually grew less violent; and by dawn on May 3, the wind had fallen off to a moderate southwesterly breeze. As noon approached, the clouds started to thin out. Before long patches of blue sky appeared, and soon the sun was shining down.

Worsley took out his sextant, and it was no task at all to get a sight. When he had worked it out, the fix put their position at 56°13' South, 45°38' West—403 miles from Elephant Island.

They were just more than halfway to South Georgia.

Thus, in the space of perhaps only an hour the outlook on board the *Caird* was completely altered. The battle was half won, and a warm sun was overhead. The off-duty watch no longer huddled in the dismal confines of the forecastle. Instead the sleeping bags were hauled out and run up the mast to dry. The men peeled off various articles of clothing, and boots, socks, and sweaters were tied onto the shrouds and backstay.

166

The sight that the *Caird* presented was one of the most incongruous imaginable. Here was a patched and battered 22-foot boat, daring to sail alone across the world's most tempestuous sea, her rigging festooned with a threadbare collection of clothing and half-rotten sleeping bags. Her crew consisted of six men whose faces were black with caked soot and half-hidden by matted beards, whose bodies were dead white from constant soaking in salt water. In addition, their faces, and particularly their fingers were marked with ugly round patches of missing skin where frostbites had eaten into their flesh. Their legs from the knees down were chafed and raw from the countless punishing trips crawling across the rocks in the bottom. And all of them were afflicted with salt water boils on their wrists, ankles, and buttocks. But had someone unexpectedly come upon this bizarre scene, undoubtedly the most striking thing would have been the attitude of the men ... relaxed, even faintly jovial—almost as if they were on an outing of some sort. By evening the sun had done a wonderful job of drying, and when they crawled into their sleeping bags that night the sensation was distinctly pleasant—at least by comparison.

The good weather held throughout the night and into the following day, May 4; and again the gear was distributed among the rigging. Worsley's sight at noon put the position at 55°31' South, 44°43' West, a run of 52 miles in twenty-four hours.

Two days of good weather had worked their magic,

and among the entire crew there was a growing feeling of confidence, subtle but unmistakable. In the beginning, South Georgia had existed only as a name—infinitely distant and lacking in reality.

But no more. They were even at this moment less than 250 miles from the nearest point on South Georgia. And having already covered 450 miles, the distance that remained was at least conceivable. Three days more, or maybe four at the most, should see them there, and then it would all be over. And so that peculiar brand of anxiety, born of an impossible goal that somehow comes within reach, began to infect them. Nothing overt, really, just a sort of added care that nothing preventable should go wrong now.

The wind remained steady out of the southeast during the night, though it grew considerably stronger, with occasional squalls to almost 40 knots. With the coming of light on May 5 a nasty, lumpy sea was running, and by nine o'clock, everything was as wet as it had ever been.

Otherwise, it was a notably uneventful day, distinguished only by the fact that toward evening the wind shifted slowly to the northwest, and by dark was blowing a gale.

At midnight, after a drink of hot milk, Shackleton's watch took over, and Shackleton himself assumed the helm while Crean and McNeish stayed below to pump. His eyes were just growing accustomed to the dark when he turned and saw a rift of brightness in the sky astern.

He called to the others to tell them the good news that the weather was clearing to the southwest.

A moment later he heard a hiss, accompanied by a low, muddled roar, and he turned to look again. The rift in the clouds, actually the crest of an enormous wave, was advancing rapidly toward them. He spun around and instinctively pulled his head down.

"For God's sake, hold on!" he shouted. "It's got us!"

For a long instant nothing happened. The *Caird* simply rose higher and higher, and the dull thunder of this enormous breaking wave filled the air.

And then it hit—and she was caught in a maelstrom of seething water and catapulted bodily forward and sideways at the same time. She seemed actually to be thrown into the air, and Shackleton was nearly torn from his seat by the deluge of water that swept over him. The lines to the rudder went slack, then suddenly seized up again as the boat was viciously swung around like some contemptible plaything.

For an instant, nothing existed but water. They couldn't even tell for sure whether she was upright. But then the instant was over; the wave had rolled on, and the *Caird,* though stunned and half dead under a load of water that rose nearly to the seats, was miraculously still afloat. Crean and McNeish seized the first implements that came to hand and began to bail furiously. A moment later, the members of Worsley's watch fought their way out of the sleeping bags and joined the struggle, throwing water over the side with a wild urgency, knowing that the next wave would surely be the finish unless they could lighten her before it struck.

Shackleton at the helm kept looking astern for another tell-tale streak of brightness. But none appeared, and ever so slowly, as they frantically pumped and bailed and ladled the water overboard, the *Caird* lifted to the seas again.

25

Where Is the Island?

THE DAWN OF MAY 6 revealed an ugly scene. The wind was blowing nearly 50 knots from the northwest, and the *Caird* was straining into it, trying to hold to a northeasterly course. As every wave passed, some portion of it poured on board the boat.

But it seemed really not to matter too much. They had been pounded and bruised and drenched almost to the point of insensibility. Furthermore, the wave during the night had somehow changed their attitude. For thirteen days they had suffered through almost ceaseless gales, then finally a huge rogue sea. They had been the underdog, fit only to endure the punishment inflicted on them.

But sufficiently provoked, there is hardly a creature on God's earth that ultimately won't turn and attempt to fight, regardless of the odds. In an unspoken sense, that was much the way they felt now. They were possessed by an angry determination to see the journey through —no matter what. They felt that they had earned it. For thirteen days they had absorbed everything that the Drake Passage could throw at them—and now, by God, they deserved to make it.

As if to mock their determination, the sea rose menacingly throughout the morning, and at one o'clock Shackleton gave the order to heave to. Then once again they began to tack back and forth into the wind.

All of them fell sullen. It seemed too much—to be so close, possibly only one good day's run, and to have to stop.

Toward dusk Crean started to prepare the evening hoosh only to discover that the second cask of water—the one that had got adrift during the launching of the *Caird* from Elephant Island—had the unmistakable brackish taste of sea water which apparently had seeped into it. Even at that more than half of the cask's contents had leaked out.

For Shackleton, the discovery meant simply that the need for haste had now become acute. It was imperative that a landing be made, and very soon, too.

The inevitable question then became—would they hit South Georgia?

Both Shackleton and Worsley knew that except for one or two tiny islands, the Atlantic Ocean eastward beyond South Georgia is a void all the way to South Africa, nearly 3,000 miles away. If, through a miscalculation or because of a southerly gale, they missed the island, there would be no second chance. The land would then lie to windward of them, and they could never beat back toward it. They dared not miss.

Fortunately, as the night wore on, the northwesterly gale diminished slightly, and the sky began to clear. At 1 A.M., Shackleton decided it was safe to get underway, and they again set their course for the northeast.

The all-important thing now was to learn the position, but soon after dawn a foglike mist moved in. They could see the sun, but only as a hazy outline. Worsley kept his sextant handy all morning, hoping that the fog would clear. After several hours, he took his notebook and, partly in desperation, he scribbled: "Most unfavourable conditions for Obs. Misty with boat jumping like a flea. . . ."

The original plan had been to round the western tip of South Georgia, then swing east and run along the coast to the whaling station at Leith Harbor. But that had assumed reasonably decent navigating conditions, and had not taken into account the shortage of water. Now it no longer mattered where they landed, just so long as they did land. So they altered course to the east, hoping to hit anywhere on the west coast of the island, and it was of very little consequence where.

It turned out, too, that the water from the broken cask was polluted with sediment and reindeer hairs. This noisome liquid had to be strained through gauze from the medicine chest; though it was drinkable—it was just barely so, and it only aggravated their thirst.

Throughout the afternoon there had been a mounting air of expectancy that they would sight some indication that the land was close by—birds or kelp or something. But there was none. And with the approach of evening, the attitude of expectancy gave way to one of apprehension—of a strangely paradoxical sort.

By Worsley's estimate they should have been a little more than 50 miles off the coast. But Worsley's calculations were admittedly crude, and they could easily have been much closer.

On the west coast of South Georgia there was not the smallest settlement, much less a beacon light or even a buoy to guide them. In fact, even to this day, the west coast of South Georgia is only sketchily charted. Thus it was entirely conceivable that they might come upon the coast in the dark—suddenly and disastrously.

On the other hand, their fear of running onto the island was oddly counterbalanced by the dread awareness that they might just as easily miss it altogether—run by it in the night, and never know it was there. Indeed, they might already have done so.

The darkness was now complete, and the *Caird* pounded forward as the men peered ahead into the night with salt-rimmed eyes for the shadowy image of a headland. At the same time they strained their ears for any unusual noise, perhaps the sound of surf pounding on a reef. But the foggy mist cut visibility almost to nothing. The only sounds that could be heard were the moaning of the wind through the stays and the surge of the heavy confused sea that was running.

Thirst, of course, heightened their expectation and prolonged each anxious minute. But in spite of the discomfort and uncertainty, there was an undercurrent of suppressed excitement. Each of the watches made wild, speculative guesses about how soon they would reach the whaling station and what it would be like to bathe and have clean clothes and sleep in a real bed and actually eat food served on a table.

174

Gradually the hours crept by, though there was nothing to indicate that they were nearing the coast. At 4 A.M., when Worsley's watch came on, Shackleton remained with him at the helm to keep a lookout for the land. They were making about 3 knots, and by six o'clock they should have been less than 15 miles offshore —but there was not a sign of it—not the smallest bit of ice or shred of seaweed.

Seven o'clock came—12 miles from the island, and yet no trace. The air of anticipation was slowly being replaced by a feeling of increasing tension. Some of the peaks on South Georgia were nearly 10,000 feet high. Surely they would be visible by now.

At eight o'clock, Shackleton's watch was due to take over. But nobody thought about watches. Instead all hands crowded into the cockpit, searching ahead and to each side in an atmosphere of competition, of hoping, of anxiety—all at once. But there was only the sea and sky, just the same as there had always been.

Toward nine o'clock, Shackleton sent Crean below to prepare some hoosh. When it was ready they ate it hurriedly in order to return to their lookout posts.

It was a strange time, a time of eagerness and expectation—underscored by grave, unspoken doubts. It was all so nearly over. An occasion for excitement, even jubilation. And yet, in the back of their minds was a nagging voice which refused to be silent—they might very well be looking in vain. If the island was there, they should have sighted it hours before.

Then, at just after ten-thirty, Vincent spotted a clump

of seaweed, and a few minutes later a cormorant was sighted overhead. Hope flared anew. Cormorants rarely ventured farther than 15 miles from land.

Soon the foggy mists began to break up, though ever so slowly. Ragged clouds still scudded along close to the surface of the water. But visibility was better. At noon the fog was almost gone. Yet the interminably heaving sea stretched in every direction.

"Land!"

It was McCarthy's voice, strong and confident. He was pointing dead ahead. And there it was. A black, frowning cliff with patches of snow clinging to its sides. It was just visible between the clouds, possibly 10 miles away. A moment later the clouds moved like a curtain across the water, shutting off the view.

But no matter. It was there, and they had all seen it.

26

So Terribly Close

SHACKLETON was the only one who spoke.

"We've done it," he said, and his voice was strangely unsteady.

Not a sound came from the others. They simply stared ahead, watching for the land to reappear, just to be sure. And it did in a minute or two, when the clouds had blown away again. Feeble, foolish grins spread across their faces, not of triumph or even joy, but simply of unspeakable relief.

By two-thirty, the *Caird* was a little more than 3 miles off the coast and it was possible to see patches of green lichens and areas of yellow-brown tussock grass showing through the snow on the steep sides of the headlands. Growing things—the first they had seen in more than sixteen months. And they would be standing amongst them in an hour or a little more.

Everything seemed perfect. But not for long. Within a few minutes, the deep rumbling sound of breakers reached them. Then dead ahead and off to the right an occasional spout of bursting spray shot skyward. As they drew closer they could see the backs of great seething combers hurtling shoreward as the Cape Horn gray-beards blindly advanced to their destruction on uncharted reefs.

The whole complexion of things was suddenly changed. There could be no thought of a landing, not here at least, for the boat would not have lived ten seconds in those breakers. It was something they didn't deserve—a needless cruelty. The land lay just in front of them, and they had earned it. Yet now that the journey was done, sanctuary was ironically denied them.

They could not even hold this course much longer. Furthermore, their incomplete chart showed no reasonable possibility of finding shelter before dark. And though by three o'clock the land was only 2 miles distant, and they could easily have reached it in less than forty-five minutes—they would have died doing so.

Thus, at 3:10 P.M., Shackleton gave the order to come about. They swung onto the starboard tack and headed seaward once again to lay off until morning in the hope that they could then make a better approach or perhaps find a way through the reefs.

They set a course for the SSE, intending to get far enough offshore so that they might safely heave to and wait for daylight. As the boat heeled to port before the following wind, hardly a one of them spoke. Individually they were fighting somehow to console their awful disappointment. But there was now, truly, but one more night to go.

Toward five o'clock the light began to fail, and the sky off the *Caird's* starboard quarter was kindled into

178

vivid, almost angry shades of orange and red that slowly faded. It was dark by 6 P.M.

Overhead a heavy bank of clouds rolled in, and the wind gradually increased, growing stronger with every hour. At eight o'clock, rain began to fall. Before long the rain turned into sleet, then hail that drummed across the decking. By 11 P.M., the storm had reached gale force, and the *Caird* was caught in a cross sea that drove in from every direction. They ran before the quartering gale until midnight; and though they had not the slightest idea where they might be, Shackleton decided they must be far enough offshore to heave to.

The remainder of that night was an eternity, composed of seconds individually endured until they merged into minutes and minutes finally grew into hours. And through it all there was the voice of the wind, shrieking as they had never heard it shriek before in all their lives.

The dawn of May 9 finally came, but there was no real dawn. Instead the wild blackness of the night slowly gave way to a thick gray pall. The wind was blowing at least 65 knots, and the cross sea was the worst it had been. Now, added to it, there was a mountainous westerly swell sweeping inland before the gale. The rollers that raced shoreward were perhaps 40 feet high, maybe more.

The *Caird,* with her miserable little rag of a trysail blown stiff by the wind, rose to the top of each onrushing swell and there she quivered before the fury of the gale. It seemed strong enough almost to peel the canvas decking off her. There, too, it was difficult even to breathe. The atmosphere was a saturated substance,

179

composed less of air than of rain and snow, and mostly wind-driven mist, torn from the surface of the water.

Visibility was reduced to a hazy sphere surrounding the boat. Beyond that was only a blinding sameness that screamed by without interruption.

And though they had not the vaguest idea where they might be, they knew one thing all too well: somewhere off to leeward the black cliffs of South Georgia were waiting, steadfastly hurling back this colossal onslaught of water.

By noon the wind was probably close to 80 knots out of the southwest. To prepare food was out of the question, but they had almost no appetites for eating anyhow. Their tongues were swollen with thirst, and their lips cracked and bleeding.

The *Caird's* bow was kept pointed into the wind. But it was astern that they looked, trying to catch a glimpse of the island or the treacherous reefs. All morning they heard them getting closer. Deep below the high-pitched shriek of the wind and the tormented upheaval of the sea, there was a thudding bass heartbeat, more felt than heard—the impact of successive waves breaking on the coast, transmitted through the water as a series of muddled shocks which struck the boat.

Then, at just about two o'clock, they saw where they were. A quirk of wind tore the clouds apart, and two wicked peaks loomed above a line of cliffs. The coastline looked to be about a mile away, perhaps a little more.

But vastly more important, in that single glimpse they saw to their terror that they were only a short distance outside the line of breakers, the point at which the seas ceased to behave like swells and became combers instead, rushing faster and faster toward their own destruction against the land. As each swell passed under them they could feel it tugging momentarily at the boat, trying to get hold of her and hurl her toward the beach. It seemed now that everything—the wind, the current, and even the sea itself—were united in a single, determined purpose—once and for all to annihilate this tiny boat which thus far had defied all their efforts to destroy it.

No choice remained but to hoist sail and try to claw their way offshore into the teeth of this fiendish gale. But it could not be done. No boat—least of all the *Caird* —could beat to windward under conditions like these.

Shackleton rushed aft and took over the lines of the tiller from Crean. Then Crean and Worsley crawled up onto the decking and pulled themselves forward on their bellies. The wind was so strong they could hardly get the jib off. McCarthy was needed to help with the mainsail, for had the wind got hold of it, the combined strength of the two men could not have kept it from being ripped out of their hands.

But at last Shackleton pulled the *Caird's* bow around to the southeast, and the wind, like a solid object, struck her a shuddering blow that all but capsized her. Shackleton shouted excitedly to McNeish and Vincent below to shift ballast. They, kneeling on the rocks and working as feverishly as their strength permitted, piled the boulders against the starboard side, and the *Caird* righted herself somewhat.

She moved forward half a boat-length before the first sea struck her and stopped her dead. Solid water was flung over the masthead, and the strain was so great that her bow planks opened up and little lines of water squirted in through the seams. Once more she moved ahead, and once more the sea clubbed her to a halt.

The water now was coming in both from above and below so fast that two men working constantly could not handle it, so Shackleton put all hands to the task.

But for all their efforts they seemed only to be standing still. Occasionally the clouds were ripped aside, revealing the coast off the port quarter, just as close as ever. After more than an hour they had demonstrated the truth of what they first suspected—it could not be done. No boat could beat to windward in such a storm.

Shackleton was sure the end was very near.

But they were wrong. Just after four o'clock, they saw that they were making headway when suddenly a rift in the storm showed a great craggy peak off the port bow. It was Annenkov Island, a 2,000-foot mountaintop shoved up out of the sea some five miles off the coast, and it lay directly in their path. There was nothing to do, however, but to hold to the southeasterly course, close into the wind, and pray God that somehow the boat could edge by the island—if the *Caird* held together that long. Neither possibility was at all likely.

By now it was getting dark, though the sky was somewhat clearer, and Annenkov Island was plainly visible most of the time as a black shape against the sky.

The sight it presented was the more awesome by contrast. While they were literally enveloped in the wild ferocity of the storm, struggling simply to remain afloat —off to port lay this huge, resolute bulk which was implacably creeping closer through the darkness. Before long they could hear the deep booming of the surf against the cliffs.

Only the man at the helm actually could see what was happening, for the others dared not pause in their bailing for fear that the water would get ahead of them. Periodically they changed tasks in order to get some relief. Thirst had long since ceased to matter, along with everything else except the fight to keep the boat under them. Each helmsman in turn, mindful of the anxiety of those below, shouted down to them reassuringly, "She'll clear it—she's doing it."

But she wasn't. By seven-thirty they were on top of the island, and the sheer mass of it now dominated everything to leeward. The sound of the seas against its side virtually drowned out even the screaming of the wind. The foaming backwash of the breakers thrown back from the cliffs swirled around the *Caird,* and the towering, snowy peak above them was so close they had to crane their necks to see it.

Worsley thought to himself of the pity of it all. He remembered the diary he had kept ever since the *Endurance* had sailed from South Georgia almost seventeen months before. That same diary, wrapped in rags and utterly soaked, was now stowed in the forepeak of the *Caird.* When she went, it would go, too. Worsley thought not so much of dying, because that was now so plainly inevitable, but of the fact that no one would ever know how terribly close they had come.

He waited at the helm, silent and tense—braced for the final, shattering impact when the *Caird's* bottom would be torn out against some unseen rock. As he watched, the water streaming down his face and dripping from his beard, the sky to the east crept into view.

"She's clearing it!" he screamed. "She's clearing it!"

The bailers stopped and everybody looked up and saw the stars shining to leeward. The island was no longer in the way. They had no idea how, even why—perhaps some unexpected eddy of the tide had driven them offshore. But no one then stopped to seek an explanation. They knew only one thing—the boat had been spared.

All at once they felt inexpressibly weary, numb, even indifferent. The gale, too, appeared exhausted by the struggle, or perhaps it knew that it had lost, for the wind rapidly died off, and within the short space of thirty minutes it had swung around to the ssw.

They came about and set a course for the northwest, giving South Georgia a wide berth. The sea was still high, but the viciousness had gone out of it.

They had to continue to bail almost until midnight before they had reduced the *Caird's* burden of water to the extent that three men could handle it. At three-thirty, Worsley's watch took over and toward seven o'clock, South Georgia came into view again, about 10 miles off to starboard.

They set a course straight for the land, but the *Caird* had hardly settled onto it when the wind fell very light.

Thus, throughout the morning, their progress was steady but painfully slow. Then about one o'clock, the tide turned and began to set against them.

The sails were lowered and, with Shackleton at the helm, the other men took turns rowing, two at a time; but they were doing little more than holding their own. However, by three o'clock, they had managed to pull close enough to see relatively calm water beyond the reefs in King Haakon Bay—and they also saw what appeared to be a safe passage. But they could not possibly get through before dark—not under oars.

It was time for a last desperate attempt. Hurriedly they ran up every sail to its full height and headed for the narrow opening in the reefs. But it meant sailing straight into the wind, and the *Caird* simply could not do it. Four times they lay off, and four times they tried to tack into the wind. Four times they failed.

It was well after four o'clock, and the light was beginning to go. They ran the *Caird* a mile to the south, trying to get the wind as much abeam as possible. Then they came about once more onto the starboard tack. This time she just managed to slip through.

Instantly the sails were dropped and the oars were put out. They rowed for about ten minutes; then Shackleton spotted a small cove in the cliffs to starboard.

The entrance was protected by a small reef of its own over which the surge of the swell was breaking. But they saw an opening—so small the oars had to be taken in at the last moment.

About 200 yards beyond was a steep, bouldered beach.

Shackleton stood in the bow, holding the frayed remains of the sea-anchor line. Finally the *Caird* rose up on a swell and her keel ground against the rocks. Shackleton jumped ashore and held her from going out.

As quickly as they could, the other men scrambled after him.

It was five o'clock on the tenth of May, 1916, and they were standing at last on the island from which they had sailed 522 days before.

They heard a trickling sound. Only a few yards away a little stream of fresh water was running down from the glaciers high above.

A moment later all six were on their knees, drinking.

27

Now . . . the Impossible

I T WAS a curiously quiet moment, almost devoid of rejoicing. They had accomplished the impossible, but at a staggering price. Now it was over, and they knew only that they were unutterably tired—too tired even to savor much more than the dim awareness that they had won. They managed, however, to shake hands all around. It seemed somehow the thing to do.

Yet even in that small moment of victory, tragedy threatened. The surf inside the cove was especially heavy. It had swung the *Caird's* stern around, and she was pounding against the rocks.

They stumbled back down the beach, but the rocks were rough and their legs were rubbery with weakness. By the time they reached the boat her rudder had already been torn off. She had to be raised clear of the water —and that meant unloading her. So they formed themselves into a chain and began the laborious job of passing the stores up the beach. When that was done the hated rock ballast was thrown over the side.

But when it came time to get the *Caird* onto safer ground, the real extent of their weakness became evident. Exerting every ounce of their combined strength, they could hardly do more than rock the boat back and forth, and after about six tries Shackleton saw that it was no use to continue until they had rested and had something to eat.

A piece of light rope was made fast to the *Caird's* bow and secured to a boulder. They left the boat at the water's edge, pounding against the rocks.

What appeared to be a small cave had been sighted about 30 yards off to the left, and they dragged their sleeping bags and a small amount of stores up to it. It proved to be hardly more than a hollow in the cliffs. But enormous icicles, at least 15 feet high, had collected across its face, forming a front wall. They crawled inside and found that the cave was about 12 feet deep, with ample room to shelter them.

Crean lighted a fire and prepared some hoosh. It was eight o'clock by the time they had finished eating, and Shackleton instructed all of them to turn in, saying that they would stand one-man watches over the *Caird*. He agreed to take the first. The others crawled into their wet, but blissfully motionless sleeping bags, and within seconds they were truly unconscious.

Everything went well until about 2 A.M. Tom Crean was on watch when a particularly heavy sea caught the *Caird* and she broke loose. Crean managed to grab the bow line and he shouted for help. But by the time the others had awakened and made their way down to the beach, Crean had been dragged into the water almost over his head.

With all of them pulling they managed to bring her

back to shore, and they tried once more to get her up the beach, this time by rolling her over. Again they lacked the strength.

They were very close to exhaustion, but even their desperate craving for sleep could not be considered when weighed against the possible loss of the boat. Shackleton decided they would have to stand by her until daylight.

They sat down to wait for morning. But there was no sleep because periodically they had to fend the *Caird* off the rocks.

Shackleton reviewed their situation in his mind. He had originally hoped to use this place only as a stopover to replenish their water and to obtain a few days' rest, then press on around the coast to Leith Harbor. But if they were to have rest, the boat had to be pulled clear of the water. To do so, they would have to lighten her by removing the decking, since they lacked the strength to lift her as she was. Once that was done, she would hardly be fit to face the sea again.

Sitting on the rocks waiting for morning, Shackleton came to the conclusion that instead of sailing to Leith Harbor, they would remain on the south side of the island and three of the party would go overland to bring help.

By sea it would have been a voyage of more than 130 miles out around the western tip of the island and then along the north coast. By land it was a scant 29 miles in a straight line. The only difference between the two was that in the three-quarters of a century that men had been coming to South Georgia, not one man had ever crossed the island—for the simple reason that it could not be done.

A few of the peaks on South Georgia rise to somewhat less than 10,000 feet, which certainly is not high by mountain-climbing standards. But the interior of the island has been described by one expert as "a saw-tooth thrust through the tortured upheaval of mountain and glacier that falls in chaos to the northern sea." In short, it was impassable.

Shackleton knew it—and yet there was no choice. He made his announcement after breakfast, and all of the men accepted it routinely and without question. Shackleton said he would make the journey with Worsley and Crean as soon as it seemed feasible.

McNeish immediately went to work removing the decking and the extra planks from the *Caird,* and by noon he had lightened her considerably. They shoved her up the beach literally by inches, pausing every few minutes to rest. She was safely above the high water mark by one o'clock.

Later in the afternoon, Shackleton and Crean climbed a plateau at the head of the cove, and there they found a number of baby albatrosses on the nest. They ate two for supper, and McNeish noted simply: "It was a treat."

Afterwards they turned in and slept for twelve glorious hours without a single interruption. By morning they all felt infinitely better. Later in the day McNeish recorded rapturously: "We have not been as comfortable for the last 5 weeks. We had 3 young & 1 old albatross for lunch. with 1 pint of gravy which beets all the chicken soup I ever tasted. I have just been thinking what our companions [on Elephant Island] would say if they had food like this."

Shackleton and Worsley, meanwhile, had made a survey of sorts around the area and saw that except for the cove in which they were camped, the cliffs and glaciers rose almost perpendicularly. Consequently, Shackleton decided they would sail the *Caird* to the head of King Haakon Bay, a distance of about 6 miles. Their chart indicated that the terrain there was somewhat more hospitable, and they would also be 6 miles closer to the opposite side of the island where the whaling stations were situated.

Short as this journey was, Shackleton felt the men were not yet equal to it, so they spent two days recuperating and eating sumptuously. May 14 had been the day set for the trip to the head of the bay, but the weather in the morning was squally with rain, so the trip was postponed until the following day. In the afternoon there were encouraging signs of clearing. McNeish wrote: "I went to the top of the hill & had a lay on the grass & it put me in mind of old times at *Home* sitting on the hillside looking down at the sea."

They were up at dawn the following morning. The *Caird* was loaded and easily shoved downhill into the water. It was an utterly carefree journey, and shortly past noon they rounded a high bluff. Before them lay a gently sloping beach populated by hundreds of sea elephants. The *Caird* was hauled up; then they turned her over, and they arranged their sleeping bags inside. It was decided to name the place "Peggotty Camp," after the poor but honest family in Dickens' *David Copperfield.*

Shackleton was extremely anxious to begin the journey, but for the next two days the weather was bad. They spent the time discussing the journey and McNeish busied himself fixing their boots for climbing. He had removed four dozen 2-inch screws from the *Caird,* and he fixed eight of them into each shoe to be worn by the members of the overland party.

The decision had been made to travel light, even without sleeping bags. Each of the overland party was to carry his own allotment of three days' sledging rations and biscuits. In addition they were to take a filled Primus stove which carried enough fuel for six meals, plus a small pot for cooking and a half-filled box of matches. They had two compasses, a pair of binoculars, and about 50 feet of rope knotted together, along with the carpenter's adz for use as an ice axe.

The only superfluous item Shackleton permitted was Worsley's diary.

The break came at dusk on May 18. The sky showed signs of clearing. Shackleton met with McNeish, whom he was leaving in charge of the three men staying behind. Shackleton gave him his final instructions, and he wrote this letter in McNeish's diary:

May 18th, 1916
South Georgia

Sir

I am about to try to reach Husvik on the East Coast of this island for relief of our party. I am leaving you in charge of the party consisting of Vincent, McCarthy & yourself. You will remain here until relief arrives. You have ample seal food which you can supplement with birds and fish according to your skill. You are left with a double barrelled gun, 50 cartridges [and other rations] ... You also have all the necessary equipment to support life for an indefinite period in the event of my non-return. You had better after winter is over try and sail around to the East Coast. The course I am making toward Husvik is *East* magnetic.

I trust to have you relieved in a few days.

Yours faithfully
E. H. Shackleton

28

Overland!

THE OTHERS TURNED IN, but Shackleton could not sleep, and he went outside repeatedly to check on the weather. It was clearing, but only very slowly. Worsley, too, got up about midnight to see how conditions were.

However, by 2 A.M., the moon was shining down brilliantly, and the air was wonderfully clear. Shackleton said the time had come.

It took only a few minutes to gather up their meager equipment. McNeish walked with Shackleton, Worsley, and Crean for about 200 yards, shook them each by the hand again and wished them luck, then walked slowly back to Peggotty Camp.

It was 3:10 A.M. The final journey had begun. Almost immediately the three men started upland, climbing a fairly steep, snow-covered slope, and they soon began to feel the strain in their legs. Fortunately, when they reached a height of about 2,500 feet the slope leveled off.

On the chart they carried, only the coastline of South Georgia was shown—and a great deal of that was missing. The interior was blank. Thus, they could be guided only by what they could see, and Shackleton was terribly eager to determine what lay ahead. But about 5 A.M., a thick fog rolled in, shrouding everything in a diffused glow of luminescence in which even the snow beneath their feet was real only when they set foot on it. Shackleton thought it would be best if they roped themselves together for safety.

By daybreak Worsley estimated that they had covered about 5 miles, and as the sun rose higher, the fog began to thin out. Peering ahead they saw an enormous snow-covered lake, just slightly to the left of their easterly course. The lake was a rare bit of good luck because it promised the opportunity of a level route across its entire length, and they started toward it.

For an hour they followed an easy downhill route, though there was an increasing number of crevasses. At first these were thin and shallow, but before long they grew wider and deeper, and it soon became apparent that the three men were descending the face of a glacier. It was an unusual situation because glaciers rarely emptied into lakes—and yet there it was, stretching invitingly before them.

By seven o'clock, however, the sun had risen high enough to burn away the last traces of the fog, and they suddenly saw that the lake extended all the way to the horizon.

They were marching toward Possession Bay—the open sea, on the northern coast of South Georgia.

They had, in fact, covered about seven miles and almost crossed the island at a narrow neck. But it was of absolutely no use to them. Even if they could have descended the perpendicular headlands below them, there was no shoreline along which they might make their way. The glacier fell sheer into the sea. Thus there was nothing to do but to retrace their steps, and they started back upland.

The worst of it was that it cost them time. Given time, they could have probed and reconnoitered for the best route, resting when they felt the need and traveling only when they were fit, and when the weather was best. But they had dared all for the sake of speed. They had neither sleeping bags nor tents. And if they were caught in these mountains by a change of weather, they would be powerless to save themselves. The blizzards of South Georgia are considered among the worst on earth.

It took two toilsome hours to regain the ground they had lost, and then they set off again toward the east. By eight-thirty they saw that a range of small mountains lay ahead, a series of ridges and spurs—four altogether, like the knuckles of a tightly clenched fist. Worsley figured that their route lay closest between the first and the second, and they set their course in that direction.

The closer they got, the steeper the ascent became, and they labored upward, a foot at a time, with Shackleton in the lead. They climbed what seemed to be an almost vertical slope, cutting steps in its face with the adz.

Finally, about eleven-fifteen, they gained the summit. Shackleton was the first to peer over, and he saw beneath him a precipitous drop, ending in a chasm 1,500 feet below. It was strewn with the shattered fragments of ice that had plunged from where he crouched. He waved for the others to come see for themselves. There was no way down. Furthermore, their way was blocked to either side, though dead ahead—the direction in which their course lay—was a gently rising snow slope, stretching away for perhaps 8 miles. It was this they had to reach—if only they could get down to it.

It had taken more than three hours of strenuous effort to reach the summit, but now the only thing to do was to retreat, to retrace their steps again and try to find a different way, perhaps around the second peak.

They granted themselves five minutes' rest, then started down the way they had come. The descent was easy and took only an hour, but it was a disheartening business. They reached the bottom at twelve-thirty and paused to have a ration of hoosh, then started up again. It was a tortuous climb, much steeper than the first, and they had to cut steps with the adz beginning halfway up the face of the slope. The height and the exertion were a terrible strain and they found it impossible to keep going steadily. Every twenty minutes or so they sprawled on their backs with their legs and arms flung out, sucking in great gulps of the rarefied air.

But finally, about three o'clock in the afternoon, they were in sight of the ridge—a cap of blue-white ice.

The view from the top revealed the descent to be every bit as frighteningly impossible as the first had been, only this time there was an added menace. The afternoon was getting on, and heavy banks of fog were beginning to form in the valley far below. Looking back, they saw more rolling in from the west.

Their situation was starkly simple: Unless they could get lower, they would freeze to death. Shackleton estimated their altitude at 4,500 feet. At such a height, the temperature at night might easily drop well below zero. They had no means for obtaining shelter, and their clothes were worn and thin.

Hurriedly Shackleton turned and started down again with the others following. This time he did his best to keep as high as possible, cutting steps in the slope and working laterally around the side of the third peak—then up again once more.

They moved as quickly as they could, but there was very little speed left in them. Their legs were wobbly and strangely disobedient.

Finally, well after four o'clock, they struggled to the top. The ridge was so sharp that Shackleton was able to sit astride it, one leg on either side. The light was fading fast, but peering warily down he saw that though the descent was steep, it was not so bad as the others had been. Toward the bottom it appeared to slope away toward level ground. But there was no telling for sure because the valley now was thick with fog and the light was very poor.

Furthermore, the fog creeping up behind them was approaching very rapidly, threatening to obliterate everything, leaving them blinded and trapped atop this razorback.

The time for hesitation was past, and Shackleton swung himself over the side. Working furiously, he began to cut steps in the face of the cliff, descending slowly, a foot at a time. A bitter chill had come into the air, and the sun was nearly down. Gradually they were getting lower, but it was maddeningly slow progress.

After thirty minutes, the ice-hard surface of the snow grew softer, indicating that the grade was not quite so steep. Shackleton stopped short. He seemed to realize all at once the futility of what he was doing. At the rate they were going it would take hours to make the descent. Furthermore, it was probably too late to turn back.

He hacked out a small platform with the adz, then called to the others to come down.

There was no need to explain the situation. Speaking rapidly, Shackleton said simply that they faced a clear-cut choice: If they stayed where they were, they would freeze—in an hour, maybe two, maybe a little more. They had to get lower—and with all possible haste.

So he suggested they slide.

Worsley and Crean were stunned—especially for such an insane solution to be coming from Shackleton. But he wasn't joking . . . he wasn't even smiling. He meant it—and they knew it.

But what if they hit a rock, Crean wanted to know.

Could they stay where they were, Shackleton replied, his voice rising.

The slope, Worsley argued. What if it didn't level off? What if there were another precipice?

199

Shackleton's patience was going. Again he demanded —could they stay where they were?

Obviously they could not, and Worsley and Crean reluctantly were forced to admit it. Nor was there really any other way of getting down. And so the decision was made. Shackleton said they would slide as a unit, holding onto one another. They quickly sat down and untied the rope which held them together. Each of them coiled up his share to form a mat. Worsley locked his legs around Shackleton's waist and put his arms around Shackleton's neck. Crean did the same with Worsley. They looked like three tobogganers without a toboggan.

Altogether it took a little more than a minute, and Shackleton did not permit any time for reflection. When they were ready, he kicked off. In the next instant their hearts stopped beating. They seemed to hang poised for a split second, then suddenly the wind was shrieking in their ears, and a white blur of snow tore past. Down . . . down . . . They screamed—not in terror necessarily, but simply because they couldn't help it. It was squeezed out of them by the rapidly mounting pressure in their ears and against their chests. Faster and faster—down . . . down . . . down!

Then they shot forward onto the level, and their speed began to slacken. A moment later they came to an abrupt halt in a snowbank.

The three men picked themselves up. They were breathless and their hearts were beating wildly. But they found themselves laughing uncontrollably. What had been a terrifying prospect possibly a hundred seconds before had turned into a breathtaking triumph.

They looked up against the darkening sky and saw the fog curling over the edge of the ridges, perhaps 2,000 feet above them—and they felt that special kind of pride of a person who in an unguarded, foolish moment accepts an impossible dare—then pulls it off to perfection.

After a bite to eat they started up the snowy slope toward the east. Within an hour a hazy glow that had silhouetted the mountain peaks rose above the ranges— the full moon, directly in their path. They kept on, guided by the light of the friendly moon, until after midnight, but their weariness was now becoming a real burden. At about twelve thirty they had reached a height of perhaps 4,000 feet and the slope leveled off, then slowly started to descend, curving slightly toward the northeast —exactly as it should toward Stromness Bay. With great expectation they turned to follow it down.

About an hour later they came in sight of the water once more. There, outlined by the moonlight, was Mutton Island, sitting in the middle of Stromness Bay. As they made their way along, other familiar landmarks came into view, and they excitedly pointed them out to one another. Within an hour or two they would be down.

But then Crean spotted a crevasse off to the right, and looking ahead they saw other crevasses in their path. They stopped—confused. They were on a glacier. Only there were no glaciers surrounding Stormness Bay.

They knew then that their own eagerness had cruelly deceived them.

Worsley took out the chart and the others gathered around him in the moonlight. They had descended to one of the many coastal indentations west of Stromness Bay. It meant that once more they had to retrace their steps. Bitterly disappointed, they turned and began to plod uphill again.

For two miserable hours they kept at it, struggling to regain the ground they had lost. By 5 o'clock they had recovered most of it, and they came to another line of ridges similar to the ones that had blocked their way the previous afternoon. Only this time there appeared to be a small pass.

But they were tired now to the point of exhaustion. They found a little sheltered spot behind a rock and sat down, huddled together with their arms around one another for warmth. Almost at once Worsley and Crean fell asleep, and Shackleton, too, caught himself nodding. Suddenly he jerked his head upright. All the years of Antarctic experience told him that this was the danger sign—the fatal sleep that trails off into freezing death. He fought to stay awake for five long minutes, then he woke the others, telling them that they had slept for half an hour.

The gap through the ridges lay perhaps a thousand feet above them, and they trudged toward it, silent with apprehension of what they would find on the other side.

It was just six o'clock when they passed through, and the first light of dawn showed that no cliff, no precipice barred the way—only a comfortable grade so far as they could see. Beyond the valley, the high hills to the west of Stromness stood away in the distance.

"It looks too good to be true," Worsley said.

They started down. When they had descended to a height of about 2,500 feet they paused to prepare breakfast. Worsley and Crean dug a hole for the Primus stove while Shackleton went to see if he could learn what lay ahead. He climbed a small ridge by cutting steps in it. The view from the top was not altogether encouraging. The slope appeared to end in another precipice, though it was hard to tell for sure.

He started down—and just then a sound reached him. It was faint and uncertain, but it could have been a steam whistle. Shackleton knew it was about 6:30 A.M. ...the time when the men at whaling stations usually were awakened.

He hurried down from the ridge to tell Worsley and Crean the exciting news. Breakfast was gulped down, then Worsley took the chronometer from around his neck and the three of them crowded around, staring fixedly at its hands. If Shackleton had heard the steam whistle at Stromness, it should blow again to call the men to work at seven o'clock.

It was 6:50 ... then 6:55. They hardly even breathed for fear of making a sound. 6:58 ... 6:59 ... . Exactly to the second, the hoot of the whistle carried through the thin morning air.

They looked at one another and smiled. Then they shook hands without speaking.

A peculiar thing to stir a man—the sound of a factory

203

whistle heard on a mountainside. But for them it was the first sound from the outside world that they had heard since December, 1914—seventeen unbelievable months before. In that instant, they felt an overwhelming sense of pride and accomplishment. Though they had failed dismally even to come close to the expedition's original objective, they knew now that somehow they had done much, much more than ever they set out to do.

They gathered up their gear, except for the Primus stove which was now empty and useless. Each of them carried one last sledging ration and a single biscuit. And so they hurried forward, floundering through the deep snow.

But 500 feet down they discovered that Shackleton had indeed seen a precipice at the end of the slope. And it was terrifyingly steep, too, almost like a church steeple. But they were in no humor to turn back now. Shackleton was lowered over the edge, and he cut steps in the icy face of the cliff. When he had reached the 50-foot limit of the rope, the other two descended to where he stood and the cycle was repeated over again. It was progress, but slow and dangerous.

It took them three full hours to make the descent, but finally, about ten o'clock, they reached the bottom. From here there was only an easy grade down into the valley, then up the other side.

It was a long climb, however, nearly 3,000 feet in all, and they were very, very tired. But with only one more ridge to go, they drove their weary bodies upward.

Finally, just at one-thirty, they gained the final ridge and stood looking down.

Spread out beneath them, 2,500 feet below, was Stromness Whaling Station. A sailing ship was tied up to one of the wharfs and a small whale catcher was entering the bay. They saw the tiny figures of men moving around the docks and sheds.

For a very long moment they stared without speaking. There didn't really seem to be very much to say, or at least anything that needed to be said.

"Let's go down," Shackleton said quietly.

The descent involved a severe, ice-covered grade, so they worked along the top of the ridge until they found a small ravine which appeared to offer a footing, and they started down. After about an hour the sides of the ravine were growing steeper and a small stream flowed down the center. As they made their way along, the stream increased in depth until they were wading through knee-deep water.

About three o'clock they looked ahead and saw that the stream ended abruptly—in a waterfall.

They reached the edge and leaned over. There was a drop of about 25 feet. But it was the only way. The ravine here had grown to the size of a gorge, and its sides were perpendicular and offered no way of getting down.

There was nothing to do but to go over the edge. With some trouble they found a boulder large enough to hold their weight, and they made one end of the rope fast to it. All three of them pulled off their Burberrys, in which they wrapped the adz, the cook pot and Worsley's diary, then pitched them over the side.

Crean was the first to go down. Shackleton and Worsley lowered him, and he reached the bottom gasping and choking. Then Shackleton lowered himself down through the water. Worsley was last.

It was an icy ducking, but they were at the bottom, and from here the ground was almost level. The rope could not be recovered, but they picked up the three articles that remained and started off for the station, now only a mile or so away.

Almost simultaneously, all three of them remembered their appearance. Their hair hung down almost to their shoulders, and their beards were matted with salt and blubber oil. Their clothes were filthy, and threadbare, and torn.

Worsley reached under his sweater and carefully took out four rusty safety pins that he had hoarded for almost two years. With them he did his best to pin up the major rents in his trousers.

29

"My Name Is Shackleton"

MATHIAS ANDERSEN was the station foreman at Stromness. He had never met Shackleton, but along with everyone else at South Georgia he knew that the *Endurance* had sailed from there in 1914 . . . and had undoubtedly been lost with all hands in the Weddell Sea.

Just then, however, his thoughts were a long way from Shackleton and the ill-fated Imperial Trans-Antarctic Expedition. He had put in a long work day, beginning at 7 A.M., and it was now after four o'clock in the afternoon and he was tired. He was standing on the dock, supervising a group of his men who were unloading supplies from a boat.

Just then he heard an outcry and looked up. Two small boys about eleven years old were running, not in play but in terror. Behind them Andersen saw the figures of three men walking slowly and with great weariness in his direction.

He was puzzled. They were strangers, certainly. But that was not so unusual as the fact that they were coming —not from the docks where a ship might come in—but from the direction of the mountains, the interior of the island.

As they drew closer he saw that they were heavily bearded, and their faces were almost black except for their eyes. Their hair was as long as a woman's and hung down almost to their shoulders. For some reason it looked stringy and stiff. Their clothing was peculiar, too. It was not the sweaters and boots worn by seamen. Instead, the three men appeared to have on parkas, though it was hard to tell because their garments were in such a ragged state.

By then the workmen had stopped what they were doing to stare at the three strangers approaching. The foreman stepped forward to meet them. The man in the center spoke in English.

"Would you please take us to Anton Andersen," he said softly.

The foreman shook his head. Anton Andersen was not at Stromness any longer, he explained. He had been replaced by the regular factory manager, Thoralf Sørlle.

The Englishman seemed pleased. "Good," he said. "I know Sørlle well."

The foreman led the way to Sørlle's house, about a hundred yards off to the right. Almost all the workmen on the pier had left their jobs to come see the three strangers who had appeared at the dock. Now they lined the route, looking curiously at the foreman and his three companions.

Andersen knocked at the manager's door, and after a moment Sørlle himself opened it. He was in his shirt sleeves and he sported a big handlebar mustache.

When he saw the three men he stepped back and a

look of disbelief came over his face.   For a long moment he stood shocked and silent before he spoke.

"Who the hell are you?" he said at last.

The man in the center stepped forward.

"My name is Shackleton," he replied in a quiet voice.

Again there was silence.   And some said that Sørlle turned away and wept.

Epilogue

THE CROSSING of South Georgia has been accomplished only by one other party. That was almost forty years later, in 1955, by a British survey team under the able leadership of Duncan Carse. That party was made up of expert climbers and was well equipped with everything needed for the journey. Even so, they found it treacherous going.

Writing from the scene in October, 1955, Carse explained that to make the crossing, two routes were available—the "high road" and the "low road."

"In distance," Carse wrote, "they are nowhere more than 10 miles apart; in difficulty, they are hardly comparable.

"We to-day are travelling easily and unhurriedly. We are fit men, with our sledges and tents and ample food and time. We break new ground but with the leisure and opportunity to probe ahead. We pick and choose our hazards, accepting only the calculated risk. No lives depend upon our success—except our own. We take the high road.

"They—Shackleton, Worsley and Crean . . . took the low road.

"I do not know how they did it, except that they had to—three men of the heroic age of Antarctic exploration with 50 feet of rope between them—and a carpenter's adze."

Every comfort the whaling station could provide was placed at the disposal of Shackleton, Worsley, and Crean. They first enjoyed the glorious luxury of a long bath, followed by a shave. Then new clothes were given them from the station's storehouse.

That night after a hearty dinner, Worsley went on board the whale-catcher *Samson* for the trip around South Georgia to Peggotty Camp where McNeish, McCarthy, and Vincent were waiting.

Shackleton, meanwhile, had arranged for the use of a large wooden whaler, the *Southern Sky,* in which to return to Elephant Island for the relief of the party there, and she sailed the following morning. Less than seventy-two hours after arriving at Stromness from across the mountains, Shackleton and his two companions sailed for Elephant Island.

It was the beginning of a maddeningly frustrating series of rescue attempts lasting more than three months, during which the pack ice surrounding Elephant Island seemed resolutely determined that no rescue ship would get through to relieve the castaways.

The *Southern Sky* encountered ice only three days out from South Georgia, and less than a week later she was forced to return to port. Within ten days, however, Shackleton had obtained from the Uruguayan government the loan of a small survey vessel, the *Instituto de Pesca No. 1,* for a second attempt to rescue his men. She limped home six days later, severely damaged by the ice through which Shackleton had tried to push her.

A third attempt was made in a balky wooden schooner, the *Emma,* which Shackleton chartered. She was at sea for nearly three weeks, during which it was a struggle merely to keep her afloat—much less to effect a rescue. The *Emma* never approached Elephant Island closer than 100 miles.

It was now August 3, nearly three and a half months since the *Caird* had sailed for South Georgia. Throughout each failure of the subsequent rescue attempts, Shackleton's anxiety had risen to the extent that Worsley said he had never seen him so on edge. He had consistently appealed to the government back in England to send a proper ice vessel to get through the pack. Now word came that the *Discovery,* which had originally carried Scott to the Antarctic in 1901, was finally on her way from England. But it would take weeks for her to arrive, and Shackleton was in no mood to sit idly by and wait.

Instead he appealed to the Chilean government for the use of an ancient sea-going tug, the *Yelcho.* He promised not to take her into any ice, for she was steel-hulled and her ability to weather the sea—much less any pack—was doubtful. The request was granted, and the *Yelcho* sailed on August 25. This time the fates were willing.

Five days later, on August 30, Worsley logged: "5.25 am Full speed . . . 11.10 [A.M.] . . . base of land faintly

visible. Threadg: our way between lumps ice, reefs, &
grounded bergs. 1.10 PM Sight the Camp to sw...."

For the twenty-two castaways on Elephant Island, August 30 began like almost any other day. At sunrise the
weather was clear and cold, giving promise of a fine day.
But before long heavy clouds rolled in and the scene once
more became, as Orde-Lees recorded, "the prevailing
gloom to which we are now so inured."

As always, almost everyone tramped individually to
the top of the lookout bluff to satisfy himself once more
that there was no ship to be seen. By now they did so
more out of habit than of hope. It was simply a ritual to
which they had become accustomed, and they climbed the
bluff without anticipation and returned to the hut without disappointment. It had been four months and six
days since the Caird had left, and there was not a man
among them who still believed seriously that she had survived the journey to South Georgia. It was now only
a matter of time until a party was sent in the Wills on
another attempted relief mission.

After breakfast, all hands got busy digging snow from
around the hut. But later in the morning the tide was
low and they decided to postpone their digging in order
to gather limpets, a small crustacean which had been
found in some numbers in the water off the spit. Wally
How was acting as cook and he was preparing a lunch of
boiled seal's backbone, a dish of which everyone had become extremely fond.

The hoosh was ready about 12:45, and except for

Marston, who had gone to the lookout bluff to make some sketches, they all gathered in the hut they had made by upending the boats.

A few minutes later they heard the artist running along the path, but nobody paid much attention. He was simply late for lunch. Then he put his head inside and spoke to Wild in a tone so breathless that some of the men thought he sounded casual.

"Hadn't we better send up some smoke signals?" he asked.

For a moment there was silence, and then, as one man, they grasped what Marston was saying.

"Before there was time for a reply," Orde-Lees recorded, "there was a rush of members tumbling over one another, all mixed up with mugs of seal hoosh, making a simultaneous dive for the door-hole which was immediately torn to shreds so that those members who could not pass through it, on account of the crush, made their exits through the 'wall,' or what remained of it."

Some put their boots on—others didn't bother. James put his on the wrong feet.

Sure enough, there was a small ship, only about a mile offshore.

Macklin dashed to the lookout bluff, tearing off his Burberry jacket as he ran. There he tied it onto the halliard of the oar that served as their flagpole. But he was only able to hoist it part of the way up before the halliard jammed. (Shackleton saw the signal at half-staff and his heart sank, he later said, because he took it to be a sign that some of the party had been lost.)

214

Hurley gathered up all the sennegrass he could find, then poured over it some blubber oil and the two gallons of paraffin they still had. He had a hard time lighting it, and when it finally ignited—almost with an explosion —it produced more flame than smoke.

But no matter. The ship was headed toward the spit.

Wild, meanwhile, had gone to the water's edge and was signaling from there the best place to send in a boat. And How had broken open a tin of precious biscuits and was offering them around. Few men, however, stopped to have one. Even so rare a treat held little appeal in the excitement of the moment.

The only invalid among them was Blackboro, whose feet had been so badly frostbitten that a portion of his left foot had been amputated. He was still in the hut and Macklin dashed back, lifted Blackboro to his shoulders, then carried him to a position on the rocks near Wild where he might better see the thrilling sight.

The ship approached to within several hundred yards, then stopped. The men ashore could see a boat being lowered. Four men got into it, followed by the sturdy, square-set figure they knew so well—Shackleton. A spontaneous cheer went up. In fact the excitement ashore was so intense that many men actually were giggling.

Within a few minutes the boat was near enough for Shackleton to be heard.

"Are you all right?" he shouted.

"All well," they replied.

Wild guided the boat to a safe place among the rocks, but because of the ice around the spit it was impossible

215

to make a landing, so the boat was held a few feet off.

Wild urged Shackleton to come ashore, if only briefly, to see how they had fixed the hut in which they had waited four long months. But Shackleton, though he was smiling and obviously relieved, was still quite noticeably anxious and wanted only to be away. He declined Wild's offer and urged the men to get on board as quickly as possible.

Certainly no great urging was needed, and one at a time they jumped from the rocks into the boat, leaving behind them without a second thought dozens of personal little items which only an hour before had been considered almost indispensable.

One load was rowed out to the *Yelcho,* and then a second.

Throughout it all Worsley had watched anxiously from the bridge of the ship.

Finally he logged: "2.10 All Well! At last! 2.15 Full speed ahead."

Macklin wrote: "I stayed on deck to watch Elephant Island recede in the distance . . . I could still see my Burberry [jacket] flapping in the breeze on the hillside—no doubt it will flap there to the wonderment of gulls and penguins till one of our familiar [gales] blows it all to ribbons."

Acknowledgments

I COULD NEVER adequately express my appreciation to all the people who contributed to this undertaking. But here, in alphabetical order, are those to whom I am particularly grateful:

William Bakewell of Dukes, Michigan.

Margery and James Fisher of Northhampton, England, co-authors of *Shackleton and the Antarctic*, who generously made available to me a great deal of the material they gathered in the preparation of their excellent and exhaustively researched life of Shackleton.

Charles J. Green of Hull, England.

Commander Lionel Greenstreet of Brixham, England.

Walter How of London, England.

Dr. Reginald W. James of Capetown, South Africa.

A. J. Kerr of Ilford, Essex, England.

James Marr of Surrey, England, who generously made available to me Frank Worsley's diary of the *Caird* boat journey for which I am especially grateful.

Dr. J. A. McIlroy of Aberystwyth, Wales.

The late Miss Cecily Shackleton, who, before her death, graciously granted me the use of her father's diary and many of his personal papers.

The Scott Polar Research Institute of Cambridge, England, and particularly Harry G. R. King and Miss Ann M. Savours of the Scott Polar Research Institute for their many hours of help and the interest they took in this project.

Arnt Wegger of the Framnaes shipbuilding firm of Sandefjord, Norway, and also Lars Christensen, Aanderud Larsen, Mathias Andersen and many others in Sandefjord.

Leonard A. Stevens of New Milford, Conn.

Sir James Wordie of Cambridge, England.

Finally, I should like to single out three individuals to whom I am especially indebted.

The first is Paul Palmer of Ridgefield, Connecticut, without whose enthusiasm, encouragement, and help this book might never have been written.

The second is Dr. Alexander H. Macklin of Cults, Aberdeenshire, Scotland, to whom I owe a debt that is difficult to express. Not only did he supply me with his own and other diaries, but he provided me with a detailed account of the boat journey to Elephant Island. His generosity, his objectivity, and most of all his patience over a period of many long months during which he painstakingly answered my numerous questions never faltered once. I called upon him for help much more than I had right to.

Finally, of my wife, I can only say that her contribution went above and beyond the call of duty.

Index

About the Author

Alfred Lansing was born and grew up in Chicago. In 1940, he cut short his studies at North Park College to join the Navy, in which he served for more than five years. He returned to college in 1946 and went to Northwestern University, where he majored in journalism.

After college, Mr. Lansing edited a weekly newspaper in Wilmette, Illinois, until 1949 when he joined the United Press, where he remained until 1952. Mr. Lansing has worked for *Collier's*, specializing in adventure stories, and since 1955 has been a free-lance writer. His articles have appeared in *Reader's Digest, Saturday Review, Collier's, Pageant, Glamour, Science Digest* and several other publications. *Endurance*, the book from which this story is derived, was Mr. Lansing's first book and was a Book-of-the-Month Club selection.

Mr. Lansing now lives with his family in Sea Cliff, New York.